THE TWENTIETH CENTURY

HAMMERSMITH & FULHAM

CHRISTINE BAYLISS & JANE KIMBER

LONDON BOROUGH OF HAMMERSMITH AND FULHAM

SUTTON PUBLISHING

First published in the United Kingdom in 1999 by
Sutton Publishing Limited · Phoenix Mill
Thrupp · Stroud · Gloucestershire · GL5 2BU

British Library Cataloguing in Publication Data
A catalogue record for this book is available from the British Library.

ISBN 0-7509-2040-8

Title page photograph: VE Day party in Dymock Street, Fulham, 1945.

The new Mayor of Hammersmith, Councillor Randolph Beresford, receiving the chain of office from the outgoing Mayor, Councillor George Simpson, 21 May 1975. In the background is the Mace Bearer, Fred Hawtin.

 ^{TM} ALAN SUTTON^{TM} and SUTTON^{TM} are the trade marks of Sutton Publishing Limited

Typeset in 11/14pt Photina.
Typesetting and origination by
Sutton Publishing Limited.
Printed in Great Britain by
Redwood, Trowbridge, Wiltshire.

Contents

This modern meeting room, known as 'The Birdcage', is one of the many attractive features of The Ark, probably the most striking building in Hammersmith. The Ark is currently tenanted by Seagram Co. Ltd, which operates in two global business segments: entertainments and spirits and wine. The building provides about 150,000 sq. ft of office space over nine floors and two basements. With plenty of natural light, suspended walkways, terraces, balconies with wonderful views, a gym and a bar for its employees, this must be one of the best places in the borough in which to work. The origin of the name relates to the boat-like structure of the building, which looms over Hammersmith Flyover rather like a ship setting out to sea.

Introduction

By 1900, the people of Hammersmith and Fulham had already experienced a century of great change and development. The twentieth century has been the era of technological advances, global warfare and the shrinking world, but the previous century had seen the dawning of the modern urban age. The two areas of Hammersmith and Fulham started the nineteenth century as a group of rural communities near the River Thames; they finished it as part of the London suburbs. Who can argue that the twentieth century has brought such a dramatic local transformation?

In the first decades of the twentieth century the borough was a crowded place. The population of Fulham was 4,428 in 1801, and had risen to 137,289 by 1901 and further to 153,284 by 1911. It peaked in 1921 at 157,938, then started to fall as the birth rate declined in the 1930s, a process accelerated by the Second World War, when people were evacuated or moved away to escape the Blitz and did not return in such numbers. Shortly before the Metropolitan Boroughs of Hammersmith and Fulham amalgamated in 1965 it was estimated at 109,000. It was a similar story in Hammersmith: 5,600 people in 1801, 112,233 in 1901, 135,523 in 1931 and 110, 147 in 1961. Many residents worked in the local industries: oil and engineering concerns along the river wharves; sweet goods industries such as Lyons, Manbré & Garton and Fullers; Fulham Gas Works and Power Station; Fulham Pottery and a host of other businesses both large and small. Other residents travelled out of the borough to their jobs each day, and the area could be characterised as a dormitory suburb of central London.

The increase in population meant that housing density in the borough was high in the early part of this century, apart from the Wormwood Scrubs area. Both Fulham and Hammersmith were largely working-class in character, and there was poverty in places such as the Avenues in Fulham and in Shepherds Bush, where in the early years of the century up to 200 people per night were sleeping out on the Green during the summer. The Hammersmith Workhouse and Infirmary were built in 1905 in Du Cane Road to cater for the indigent and the infirm sick. But there was also a significant middle-class presence, and it was not until the 1920s that the Labour Party began to be represented in local politics. Unemployment, although high after the First World War and during the Depression, was never as big a problem here as in some parts of the country, due to the number of industries available locally. By 1920 only two other boroughs in London had a lower proportion of the population in receipt of poor relief than Fulham. Overcrowding and lack of domestic amenities such as bathrooms were the main problems, which the local authorities and the London County Council tackled from the early years of the century onwards through slum clearance and the erection of public housing. The Metropolitan Borough of Hammersmith was quicker to do this, and enjoyed the advantage of vacant land in the north of its area, on and adjoining the former White City exhibition site. In Fulham the challenge was to find any suitable land for building, and the Council had its eye on the Hurlingham Club polo grounds for many years, finally building Sulivan Court on part of the grounds in the 1950s. Even after the Second World War Fulham Council preferred not to erect high-rise dwellings, which it felt would be inappropriate to the area.

The London Government Act of 1899 established the Metropolitan Boroughs of Fulham and Hammersmith in place of the Vestries, whose functions the Borough Councils took over and expanded. The boroughs were by then densely populated and urbanized, and their people needed new municipal amenities and services. The earliest public library was opened in Fulham in 1887, and the central libraries, still the main libraries in the borough, were opened in 1905 (Hammersmith) and 1909 (Fulham). Fulham Public Baths and Washhouses were built in 1902 and the Public Baths at Lime Grove opened in 1908. Public health and welfare improved as maternity clinics, school clinics and children's and old people's homes were established by the Council and the London County Council, and as the old workhouse hospitals developed into general hospitals, including Fulham Hospital (now Charing Cross Hospital) and Hammersmith Hospital. By 1900 the School Board for London had already built a number of primary schools to cater for the increased local population of children. The London County Council built secondary schools after 1904, and technical schools, adult education institutes and colleges were also developed. The overcrowded locality needed public parks as breathing spaces for its residents, in addition to surviving pieces of common land such as Wormwood Scrubs and Eelbrook Common which had escaped building development. Parks laid out in this century include South Park, Hurlingham Park (which had originally been Hurlingham Club's No. 1 Polo Ground and was used as allotments during the Second World War), Wormholt Park and Furnivall Gardens. In 1965 the Metropolitan Boroughs of Hammersmith and Fulham were amalgamated to form the London Borough of Hammersmith, renamed the London Borough of Hammersmith and Fulham in 1979 as a result of pressure from Fulhamites. The London County Council became the Greater London Council at the same time, while the Inner London Education Authority, which managed schools in the borough, was formed as a successor body to the educational function of the LCC. Both the GLC and ILEA were abolished by the government in 1986, at which time their responsibilities in this area, including schools, some parks and some housing, were handed back to the borough.

Parallel to the development of municipal services, the twentieth century has seen the growth of mass entertainment to cater for people's leisure needs, and some important venues have been located in the borough. The exhibitions and spectacles at the White City, Olympia and Earls Court before 1914 represented the last flowering of the Edwardian age of leisure and unlimited labour resources, soon to be swept away by the First World War. Although the White City has gone, the two other venues have managed to survive by adapting to modern conference and show requirements. The Lyric Theatre, originally opened in 1888, had its finest hour between 1918 and 1933, when Nigel Playfair was owner/manager, and continues to provide good theatre, as do the Bush Theatre and Riverside Studios Theatre. Other well-known local theatres included the Grand and the

Granville in Fulham and the King's Theatre and the Shepherds Bush Empire in Hammersmith, of which only the last survives, as a rock music venue. A striking phenomenon of the 1920s and '30s was the popularity of cinema-going, when half of the population used to visit the cinema at least once a week. All the cinemas in the borough have now closed or been converted to other uses, except the Virgin Cinema in King Street. Television, which was largely responsible for cinema's demise, has been closely identified with the borough through the BBC Studios in Lime Grove and BBC Television Centre in White City. Hammersmith Palais, opened in 1919, was for three generations the scene of many local courtships on its famous dance floor. Sports facilities have included the White City Stadium, where the 1908 Olympic Games were held, the West London Stadium (now Linford Christie Stadium), and the Janet Adegoke Leisure Centre.

The two World Wars changed the face of British society. Soldiers returning from the First World War needed not only jobs but also houses, which stimulated the local authorities and charitable organizations to build affordable dwellings. The air raids of the Second World War claimed lives, destroyed property and caused population movement. Many mothers and children were evacuated from the borough, certain local road and development projects which had been planned were delayed, and after the war reconstruction was needed. The Irish community, already well established in Hammersmith and Fulham, increased as workers came over from Ireland, and they were joined from the 1950s onwards by people from the Caribbean. A number of Polish servicemen also settled in Hammersmith and other parts of west London after the war.

The post-war period has seen a marked decline in the local population. Between 1951 and 1961 the borough's population fell by 8 per cent, a further 16 per cent in the next decade and 21 per cent between 1971 and 1981. The main reason for this decline seems to have been that, as standards of living improved and households required larger space in which to accommodate themselves, the amount of available dwellings proved insufficient and there was migration away from the borough. The fall in population may have been hastened by the closure of many local industries in the 1960s and '70s, especially along the river frontage and wharves. Firms were squeezed out by pressure for residential and retail land, traffic congestion which made transport of goods difficult, and national decline in the manufacturing sector. The main employers in the borough are now office-based businesses and services, the local authority, the National Health Service, and the BBC and other leisure providers. There were still 2,000 families on the waiting list for council housing in Fulham in 1962, and municipal housing continued to be built until the 1980s, when government legislation brought it almost to an end. Owner-occupation has also increased in the borough, but the private rented sector has declined dramatically. The most striking post-war change in Fulham and parts of Hammersmith has been the purchase of dwellings originally built for the working classes and their conversion into expensive properties, a process of gentrification which has brought with it smart bars, restaurants and shops. The Piccadilly Line now links Hammersmith with Heathrow, and major east–west roads slice through the borough. The Westway was completed as a through road in 1932, but was upgraded to a motorway in 1966–70, and the Hammersmith flyover carrying the A4 past St Paul's Church was opened in 1961. Around the flyover, the Queen Caroline Street and Hammersmith Broadway areas have been extensively redeveloped since the 1960s, with buildings such as Hammersmith House and the Novotel hotel, and more recently with the Centre West office development, the Ark and the rebuilding of Hammersmith tube and bus stations.

What lies in the future for the London Borough of Hammersmith and Fulham? The census data for 1991 tells us part of the story. The population of 148,502 is predicted to rise by 4 per cent by 2016, during which period the present 20 per cent proportion of people from ethnic minorities will remain steady. In 1991 the overall economic activity rate in the borough was among the highest in London, and is projected to continue rising as more women join the workforce. In all, 72 per cent of dwellings in the borough are flats, and single person and single parent households will probably continue to increase, following general trends in society. Standards of living are far higher than they were when the century opened, but nevertheless there are pockets of unemployment and deprivation, for instance on the White City estate and in Shepherds Bush, which will continue to present a challenge to the local authority. It is likely that traffic congestion and pollution will be an important issue for the borough after the millennium. The major multi-national firms, such as Walt Disney, Seagram, Coca-Cola, United International Pictures, United Distillers and HarperCollins, that have chosen to site their headquarters in central Hammersmith, bring a certain prestige to the area. Two examples of good modern architecture, the Ark building in Talgarth Road and the warehouse on the river converted by Richard Rogers for his offices, attract sightseers from outside the borough. The presence of three professional football clubs will also keep the borough on the map as long as football continues to be so popular. The new shopping and leisure development at White City promises to be exciting. Hammersmith and Fulham people will, as always, be living with change for the foreseeable future.

Acknowledgements

All the pictures in this book have been selected from the collection of more than 60,000 photographs held at Hammersmith and Fulham Archives and Local History Centre. Thanks are offered to the following for granting permission to reproduce certain photographs in the book, with apologies for any omissions: in particular to the *Hammersmith, Fulham and Shepherds Bush Gazette*; and also to the BBC Photograph Library, *The Bath Chronicle*, Christine Bayliss, Christopher L. Bayliss, *Daily Graphic, Daily Mail*, Greyhound Racing Association, Hammersmith & West London College, Mr and Mrs J. Martin, Metropolitan Police Historical Museum, Museum of London, North Thames Gas Board, Paddy Fahey (Grange Museum), Seagram Co. Ltd, Sunlight Laundry, Terry Austin-Smith, Tesco Photographic Unit, The '600' Group, United Biscuits, *Weston & Somerset Mercury*.

The authors would also like to thank colleagues at Hammersmith and Fulham Reference Libraries for their assistance.

Chapter 1
Getting About

Some of the vehicles used by the Drayton Paper Works Co. in the 1930s. The company, founded in 1856, moved from Southwark to purpose-built premises in Sulivan Road, Fulham, in 1913/14. In its early days the company pioneered in the UK the production of toilet paper in roll form rather than single sheets fastened together at one corner. It also produced a range of papers and printed items. In the 1930s the company decided to adopt a five-day working week, apparently with resulting enthusiasm and efficiency in all departments. It took delivery of its first motor lorry in 1914, to complement its existing fleet of horse-drawn vehicles.

By the beginning of the twentieth century, the introduction of buses, trams and railways in Hammersmith and Fulham had already encouraged housing development and therefore population growth. A significant number of people were also employed locally in connection with the transport infrastructure, such as employees of the London General Omnibus Co. (LGOC), which had offices and garages at 101 Farm Lane, Fulham, and thousands of railway workers.

In early days public transport in the borough was by stagecoach, mail coach or hackney coach drawn by horses, or by boat on the Thames. The building of Fulham and Hammersmith Bridges, the eventual abolition of tolls on roads and bridges and the abolition of the hackney carriage monopoly in central London opened the way for the development of a public transport network. The earliest form of mass public transport along existing roads was the horse bus, introduced in London in 1829 by George Shillibeer. By the end of the century many of the smaller private bus companies in London had been taken over by the LGOC, which, together with its rival the London Road Car Co. (LRCC), maintained a number of stables for its horses in the borough. R.F. Miller, a Hammersmith man, designed the standard knifeboard type of early bus for the LGOC in 1856. Horse buses began to be replaced by motor buses in the early years of this century, and the changeover became inevitable when the horses were required for service in the First World War. The LGOC's first standardized motor bus, the 'B' type, was built partly at coach works in Olaf Street and Seagrave Road. A number of independent or pirate buses operated in the 1920s and '30s until the formation of the London Passenger Transport Board (LPTB) brought an end to competition in 1933. By 1950 the petrol-driven bus had been withdrawn and all buses were powered by diesel. In recent years the reintroduction of competition between bus operators has not affected London as much as it has provincial towns.

The first tram route in the area opened in 1874, passing along the Uxbridge Road, and by the end of the nineteenth century there were numerous tram companies. Trams were smoother than buses and the horses could haul a larger load on rails than on uneven road surfaces, but laying and repairing the track was expensive. Trams ran along Fulham Palace Road but were never introduced into central Fulham, as the streets around Walham Green were too narrow. By 1910 most of the London tram routes had been taken over by the London County Council (LCC), which had a tram depot in Great Church Lane (now Talgarth Road), and by 1915 all the tramway routes had been electrified, the first being at Shepherds Bush and Hammersmith in 1901. Like the buses, trams were taken over in 1933 by the London Passenger Transport Board, which began to convert tramways to trolleybus operations. The first trolleybuses to run through the borough arrived in the mid-1930s, but conversion of the routes was halted by the Second World War. The diesel bus then triumphed over both trams and trolleybuses, which ceased to run in London in 1952 and 1962 respectively.

The overground railway arrived when, after a short-lived earlier attempt, the West London Railway/West London Extension Railway opened successfully in 1862/3, running from the south-eastern corner of the parish of Fulham up through White City and Wormwood Scrubs to Willesden Junction, where a station opened in 1866. Several stations on the line, which is now mainly used for freight, closed in 1940 and never reopened, including Chelsea and Fulham, Uxbridge Road, and St Quintin Park and Wormwood Scrubs. The defunct London & South Western Railway had stations at Shepherds Bush and Hammersmith (Grove Road) which were demolished after the railway ceased operation in 1916. Other railways passed through the borough, and the area of Hammersmith north of Old Oak Common in particular became criss-crossed with railway tracks, sidings and junctions. Fulham had no railways apart from the West London Railway.

From the 1860s underground railways quickly became a convenient form of transport. In Fulham the District Line (then the Metropolitan District Railway) was extended to Hammersmith via West Kensington in 1874, and to Putney Bridge in 1880. Some existing railway stations were used; others such as Barons Court (1905) and Stamford Brook (1912) were added later. Fulham Broadway station was originally called Walham Green, but the name was changed in 1951 after people complained that there were no stations in the area which incorporated the name Fulham in their title. Hammersmith, always better served by public transport, has several tube lines. The Hammersmith & City Line (formerly the Metropolitan Railway) was extended to Hammersmith in 1864. Shepherds Bush and Goldhawk Road stations were built in 1914, but Wood Lane station closed the same year except for special occasions at White City. The first modern deep tube railway was the Central London Railway, later renamed the Central Line and nicknamed the Twopenny Tube, which opened eastward from Shepherds Bush in 1900. The Piccadilly Line opened from Hammersmith to Finsbury Park in 1906, and was extended to Uxbridge and Hounslow West in 1933 and to Heathrow in 1977, thus creating a fast link to the airport which has encouraged international firms to site their London headquarters in Hammersmith.

The most striking transport development in the borough this century has been the huge growth in use of motor vehicles and the building of new roads and roundabouts to accommodate the flow of traffic along the western London routes. A major road out of London had been planned since the First World War, and the Hammersmith flyover, which now carries the A4 past the Hammersmith Broadway Centre and St Paul's Church, was finally opened in 1961. It has had the unfortunate effect of creating one of the most polluted spots in London near where many people work and shop. Further north, the Westway between White City and Paddington and the first section of the West Cross Route opened in 1970. The Westway carries a motorway, the A40(M), almost into the heart of London, and has had a lasting effect on the appearance and culture of that part of the borough.

On 17 June 1905 the Prince of Wales inaugurated a new steamboat service for the LCC between Hammersmith and Greenwich. Thirty boats were put into service, some of which can be seen here from Upper Mall looking towards Hammersmith Bridge in about 1907. Several Hammersmith borough councillors travelled to the ceremony on board the *Morris*, named after the late William Morris, a famous Hammersmith resident. The service, which ran at 15-minute intervals, was unsuccessful and was discontinued in October 1907 having incurred losses of nearly £163,000. The City Steamboat Co. purchased some vessels, but steamboat services ceased at the outbreak of war in 1914. A new service was inaugurated in 1948 but it and its successors have also failed.

Three days' continuous rain in June 1903 brought disruption to residents in both Fulham and Hammersmith as the drains in low-lying areas proved inadequate to cope with the downpour. At Hammersmith Station, on the District Line, the water flooded the line along nearly the whole length of the platform and came to within 1 ft of the top of it. Water also filled the tunnel, necessitating a slow journey up the steep incline to Ravenscourt Park Station with water nearly up to the trains' footplates. Many photographers took the opportunity of recording the flooding and this dramatic view was published in *Pearsons Magazine* the following year as a reminder of events of the previous summer.

Passengers on this bus bound for Fulham and Hammersmith on 2 February 1909 were delayed when a 24 in water main in the lower section of Putney High Street burst at one of its joints, in the middle of the rush hour. The water rose several feet in the air and for a moment the fully laden motor bus seemed to be in great danger. Luckily the 'whirling flood' rushed into the Thames, averting a tragedy. Pedestrians waded through 2 ft of water and the bus passengers had to be rescued by boat. After the water had subsided it was seen that the roadway had been torn up for 200 yd by the force of the explosion.

A busman's funeral procession viewed from the bus garage at Hammersmith Broadway opposite St Paul's Church, possibly in 1914. Bus drivers walk behind the wreath-covered bus followed by their conductors, together with a crowd of interested onlookers. The identity of the deceased is unknown, but it may have been the unfortunate Andrew Hill who died on 2 April 1914 following an accident on 21 March when he fell from a ladder into a tank of boiling caustic soda, while doing a cleaning job at Hammersmith Bus Garage. A verdict of accidental death was recorded at the inquest, but no report of his funeral was published in local newspapers.

George Shillibeer introduced horse buses into London in 1829. Numerous small omnibus companies sprang up and by the 1850s there were 810 in London alone. A large number of stables were maintained in Fulham and Hammersmith by the London General Omnibus Company and the London Road Car Company, as well as by many of the smaller operators. Over 60 buses were housed and 700 horses were stabled at the Farm Lane yard owned by the LRCC. In the 1890s, the horses cost about £35 each and worked for five years from the age of five. It took about eight weeks to train them and they were expected to pull a load of 3–4 tons. There was intense competition between the companies that ran regular advertised schedules and 'pirates' which ran when and where fares were likely to be found. Accidents were not uncommon. Horse buses started to be withdrawn early in the century as motor bus services were introduced, and some of the old stables continued in use as motor garages. The view above shows a horse bus stand outside Peterborough Arms public house (now Southern Cross) in New Kings Road, summer 1904. Below is a view of North End Road Market near North End Road School, with horse buses and carts, taken for the *Fulham Borough Guide* published in 1905.

The LCC introduced tram services in Fulham from 23 January 1909. An existing route between Willesden Junction and Hammersmith Broadway was extended to Putney Bridge via Fulham Palace Road, where this photograph was taken. No alternative routes were viable, as the streets in central Fulham were too narrow to accommodate the trams. Many old and (according to today's taste) attractive properties on the western side of Fulham High Street had to be demolished when widening was carried out. Four years later, in 1912, the route was further extended to Putney Bridge Road in Wandsworth and later still to Garrett Lane, a route very similar to today's 220 bus service.

The Hammersmith section of the Grand Union Canal, crossing east–west across Wormwood Scrubs, was formerly part of the Grand Junction Canal opened between Paddington and Southall in 1801. Canals originally provided a cheap and direct route to London from the industrial cities of the Midlands, but declined after the coming of the railways. However, in recent years canals, which since 1962 have been the responsibility of the British Waterways Board, have been seen as an environmental and recreational amenity. In 1973 it was decided to plant trees to hide industrial development on the north side of the canal, and here some of the 10 tons of topsoil brought in by barge are being prepared for tree planting.

A view of the platforms at Walham Green, 1890. This station on the Metropolitan District Line was opened on 1 March 1880, after the line had been extended from West Brompton to Putney Bridge, enabling passengers to travel directly to Mansion House and intermediate stations. On the same day a new service was opened from Hammersmith to the City which ran at 10-minute intervals and two additional workmen's trains were introduced which left at 5.23 a.m. and 5.53 a.m. and arrived at Aldgate 44 minutes later. Staff at the four stations on the extended line won the Courtesy Shield in 1932, in competition with all stations on the District Line. The station was renamed Fulham Broadway in 1952.

A train of old Inner Circle 'C' stock, on the Kensington High Street–Olympia service, photographed at Kensington Olympia Station during an exhibition held, *c.* 1950. Several railway companies, including the London & South Western Railway and the West London Extension Railway, used the station, which had mixed fortunes. Opened in May 1844, it closed six months later as there were few services, fewer passengers and a loss of £50 a week. The station was rebuilt in 1861 and reopened the following year. More recently, between 1965 and 1983, part of the station was used as one of the London termini for the Motorail service to Scotland. Today services are provided for both underground and main line passengers.

A trolleybus in Hammersmith Broadway on route 628, which started in 1937 and ran from Craven Park to Clapham Junction via Fulham Palace Road. The first trolleybus services between Hammersmith, Hounslow and Hampton Court started on 27 October 1935. They used the overhead equipment that had powered the trams, but didn't require the high-maintenance metal tram tracks. They also had the advantage of being able to pull into the side of the road, and were much quieter than trams. In 1954 London Transport announced that trolleybuses were to be phased out in favour of the diesel bus, the newly designed Routemaster. The last trolleybus service in London ran on the night of 8/9 May 1962.

When this photograph of Fulham Palace Road was taken in 1938 there was much concern about the state of the road and the consequent hazards to traffic, particularly the tramway tracks which had been obsolete since trolleybuses were introduced on 12 September 1937. The London Passenger Transport Board gave notice that they would abandon the tracks at the end of November and Fulham Borough Council was left with the job of removing the tracks and resurfacing the road between Yeldham Road and Putney Bridge. As the LPTB was not prepared to pay the full cost of restoration, the case was taken to arbitration where the Council was awarded £13,204 against the board's offer of £5,687. The amount claimed by the Council was £17,366.

A quiet day in Fulham Broadway, looking towards Harwood Road, early 1950s. Traffic seems almost non-existent, with a high ratio of commercial and public transport to privately owned cars. In those days the side streets were free of parked cars, enabling children to play games of marbles in the road on their way home from school. Eventually the growth of private car ownership forced parking restrictions of various kinds. Fulham Borough Council decided in 1963 not to install parking meters, even though there were parking problems in some parts of the borough, especially near the tube stations where commuters left their cars. The first parking meters in the borough finally came into operation on 1 April 1969.

This dramatic photograph, taken on 7 November 1960 looking west from the tower of St Paul's Church, was one of a series commissioned by Hammersmith Libraries to show the progress of work on the construction of Hammersmith Flyover and associated roads. A major road out of west London had been planned since before the First World War. The flyover, which crossed several roads and the District and Piccadilly lines, opened on 16 November 1961, some 21 months after work started. The precast concrete structure, which carries the A4, is 2,831 ft long overall and 61 ft wide, and an electrically heated road surface was incorporated to stop ice forming in the winter months.

This photograph, published in the *Shepherds Bush Gazette* on 6 August 1970, shows the Westway roundabout at the White City junction. The new highway between Paddington and White City was part of the A40 trunk road to South Wales. Work began on 'Britain's longest elevated highway' (2½ miles) in September 1966 and was completed on time four years later at a cost of over £33 million. The official opening of Westway and the first section of the West Cross Route between White City and Holland Park Avenue took place on 28 July 1970. Clearly not everyone was happy about the road, as there were protests at the opening about the traffic noise, and demands for local residents to be rehoused.

Chapter 2
A Roof Over One's Head

The 4 ton complete circle crane with a 60 ft tower and 100 ft jib used in the construction of the Lisgar Terrace flats, photographed in 1927. When Samuel Lewis, a self-made man, died in 1901 he left a sum of £400,000 from his £4 million estate for the 'erection of suitable dwellings to be let to poor persons'. These were to be managed in a similar way to those of the Guinness Trust, which was already building homes for the poor. A further £250,000 was added to this sum on the death of his wife in 1906. The first estate was built in Islington in 1910; later, estates were built in Vanston Place (1922) and Lisgar Terrace (1928).

The building development of Fulham was nearing completion by 1900. Local builders had been very active in Fulham since the 1870s, including Jimmy Nichols, who built the Peterborough Estate in the early 1890s, and the partnership of Gibbs and Flew, who teamed up in 1876 and built the Margravine, Fulham Park, Munster Park and several other residential developments. Mansion blocks continued to be built in Barons Court after the turn of the century, and smaller houses for the working classes were still being put up until the First World War, especially on the Sulivan and Crabtree estates. In the decades after the First World War further blocks of flats were built, such as those on the site of North End House (demolished in 1927), West Kensington Court nearby and Parkview Court, 1933, in Fulham High Street.

Returning servicemen in 1918 needed 'homes fit for heroes', and the comparatively high level of employment in local industries exacerbated the shortage of housing. The War Seal Mansions in Fulham Road, now known as Sir Oswald Stoll Mansions, were founded in 1916 for disabled ex-servicemen. There were notorious slums in 'The Avenues' (Rock, Grove, Walham and Lodge Avenues), with 10 or 11 people occupying each house, and a survey of 1931 found that nearly half the houses in Fulham, many of which lacked bathrooms, housed more than one family. The Housing of the Working Classes Act 1890 and the Housing Act 1919 had enabled local authorities to build and manage municipal housing, but Fulham Metropolitan Council was slow to do this, and a Housing Committee was not formed until 1924. The first Council housing development was in Wyfold Road, opened in 1926. Fulham Court, on the Swan Brewery site, followed in 1933. By then the Peabody Trust, the Samuel Lewis Trust and the Fulham Housing Association had already been active and had built 823 flats. By the outbreak of the Second World War The Avenues had been cleared, and between 1937 and 1939 several new blocks of flats were built named after Labour pioneers, including Hardie, Morris, Parnell and Owen. The air raids of the Second World War destroyed some 1,134 houses in Fulham and damaged 30,000 others, so there was again a shortage of housing after the war, despite the fact that the population had fallen. The Council continued with its slum clearance and building programmes, and the period from the 1950s to the 1970s saw the peak of Council house building. By 1962 the Council owned more than 4,000 dwellings, or about one-eighth of the housing stock in Fulham. Some of the blocks of flats were high-rise, such as Clem Attlee Court (16 storeys), opened in 1957 by Earl Attlee, although the area was not suitable for large tower block developments. Another post-war estate was Sulivan Court, built 1950–6 on the former No. 2 polo ground at Hurlingham Club. By 1963 more than 1,600 post-war municipal dwellings had been erected in Fulham.

The most upmarket parts of Hammersmith were on the riverfront around Upper and Lower Mall, St Peter's Square, Ravenscourt and Stamford Brook. In central Hammersmith the terraces were grander than in Fulham, sometimes three to five storeys high, and a large proportion of them were owned by private landlords who divided them into flats and rented them out. The Wormwood Scrubs area was still rural in 1914, and the northern part of Hammersmith was the last part of the borough to be developed. Hammersmith Metropolitan Borough Council was faced with the same problem of slum clearance as its counterpart in Fulham, but it was quicker to deal with it, and formed the Housing,

Improvements and Development Committee in 1919. The first housing built by the Council was 24 workmen's tenements at Yeldham Road, opened in 1904, and its first major housing development was the Wormholt estate, where 590 houses were built in the early 1920s. The estate was partly for ex-servicemen, and 99-year leases on the properties were made available for sale to prospective tenants – an early example of 'right to buy', although take-up was disappointing. Another project was the reconstruction of the Creek area in south Hammersmith, where in 1891 one of the streets (Trafalgar Street) had contained 213 people living in 22 houses. A large estate housing 364 families was erected by the Guinness Trust at the northern end of Fulham Palace Road at the turn of the century. The London County Council (LCC) also provided housing, such as the Old Oak Estate, a cottage estate of some 1,055 dwellings built between 1912 and 1927 and currently being refurbished. In the late 1930s the LCC built the White City Estate on land formerly occupied by part of the White City, naming streets after some of the countries of the British Empire. Slum clearance continued into the 1960s, and overcrowding remained a problem until then, but gradually population density fell as new housing stock replaced Victorian dwellings.

When the London Borough of Hammersmith and Fulham was formed in 1965, it also became the primary housing authority within its area. By 1979 the Greater London Council had transferred all its housing stock to the boroughs, and at the same time the government began to curb spending on Council housing. The 1980 Housing Act allowed the sale of Council houses to tenants. In recent years the emphasis has been on refurbishment rather than new building and on the establishment of conservation areas in parts of the borough which have attractive houses. In certain cases, for example on the Clem Attlee estate, improvements have meant the demolition of some of the blocks of flats. In many streets in Fulham houses which were formerly intended for the working classes have been renovated by their owners and are now fetching high prices. Expensive new houses and blocks of private flats are going up wherever developers can find space and planning permission, prime examples being the Chelsea Harbour development and developments on the sites of Cadby Hall, the Western Hospital and Fulham Power Station. The process of gentrification in Fulham has not yet touched most parts of Hammersmith, apart from one or two desirable localities such as Brook Green and Stamford Brook. The 1991 census data shows that there are 73,568 dwellings in the borough – a 10 per cent increase on the 1981 total – of which three-quarters are flats. Owner-occupation has increased from 30 per cent of households in 1981 to 42 per cent in 1991. Only 4 per cent of households lack exclusive use of basic amenities, and overcrowding is also declining. The story of housing in the twentieth century in this borough has a relatively happy ending.

King Edward's Mansions in Fulham Road, opposite the junction with North End Road, *c.* 1910. They were described by an estate agent in 1985 as a 'Victorian mansion block', but in fact the flats were designed by Messrs Palgrave & Co. in 1905, four years after the death of Queen Victoria, and named after the reigning monarch King Edward VII. They were built on the site of Berwick House, used as the offices of the Fulham Vestry from about 1866–90. Claude Grahame-White, the well-known aviator and aircraft manufacturer, occupied flat no. 23 in the mansions 1908–11.

Heckfield Place, Fulham, 2 May 1931. Heckfield Place was part of an area known as 'The Avenues' which included Walham Avenue, Lodge Avenue and Rock Avenue. In 1937 Fulham Borough Council declared that 150 properties in The Avenues were unfit for human habitation, and that they should be compulsorily purchased, demolished and the sites redeveloped. It was proposed to rehouse the 1,415 people living there either in the new development or nearby. Proposals included a much-needed social centre, day nursery and clinic and an extension to the police station. Unfortunately the plans did not come to fruition until several years after the Second World War.

These slums in New Street, a tiny turning between Doves Place and Hampshire Hog Lane, were photographed in 1929. The street was finally demolished in 1935 as part of Hammersmith Borough Council's Southern Improvement Scheme, a slum clearance programme in an area round The Creek where the buildings were described in 1918 as being of 'an insanitary and unsuitable character'. It took some time to acquire the land, and work on the construction of Riverside Gardens was delayed until 1928. Hammersmith Town Hall was built on part of the site after The Creek had been culverted. The Second World War intervened and plans for the area changed with the building of the Great West Road over the site of New Street.

Somerset Place was a narrow thoroughfare off Lower Mall, just to the east of Hammersmith Bridge and running parallel to Hammersmith Bridge Road. As can be seen in this undated photograph, the houses were tiny with only a short front garden and a minute yard at the back. The need to find homes for bombed-out families during the Second World War accentuated housing difficulties in the borough, especially as the number of housing units available had declined because of the bombing. After the war the LCC developed the large estate known as Caroline Estate, just to the north of Somerset Place, naming all the blocks after Queens of England.

Rowton House, the 'newest poor man's hotel', opened in Hammersmith on 30 November 1899. The building, the fourth Rowton House in London, was designed by H.P. Measures and provided 800 sleeping cubicles for men at a cost of 6*d* (2½p) a night. Cooking facilities were provided or meals could be purchased on the premises, there were spacious washrooms (seen here in 1899), cupboards for drying clothes, a smoking room, a hall where draughts and chess could be played, lockers and a library. The Houses provided homes and security for those on a low income and for a number of disabled men. The Hammersmith House closed in 1972 but little alternative provision was made for the homeless men.

The Hutments in Wood Lane just to the north of the White City Exhibition grounds, photographed here in 1919, were part of Hammersmith's answer to the housing problem after the end of the First World War. The Council paid £8,500 to W.E. Blake Explosive Loading Co. Ltd for a number of wartime munitions huts, and converted them into living accommodation for 50 ex-servicemen and their families. Basic services were already provided, and it was only necessary to install a gas cooker in each new home, plus a central bathhouse and washhouse and a small garden for the complex. The Hutments were officially opened on 14 August 1919 and continued in use for about eight years.

Fulham's first venture into municipal housing was relatively late compared to Hammersmith's, as it was thought that provision of Council housing was impractical owing to the high cost of land and the work involved. The borough's first Housing Committee was formed only in 1924 and little time was wasted in constructing a small development of 18 three-bedroom and 18 two-bedroom flats in Wyfold Road, designed by the Borough Surveyor, A.F. Holden. The foundation stone of the flats was laid on 2 February 1926 by Councillor Frank Holmes, and the first flats were ready for occupation a few months later. The final cost of the scheme was £18,476.

The scarcity of land in Fulham presented the Council with difficulties in fulfilling its housing obligations. One solution was to convert pairs of soundly built old houses into flats with all modern conveniences. To publicize what could be done, show houses were opened in Cedarne Road (pictured here) and local residents invited to inspect the changes. The exhibition, which ran for three weeks, was opened by the Minister of Housing, Henry Brooke, on 24 March 1958. By cutting through the party walls and removing one of the staircases it was possible to gain enough space to install bathrooms and toilets, and in addition the scheme made it possible for the flats to be self-contained.

Former Prime Minister Earl Attlee opens the first blocks of Clem Attlee Court on 21 September 1957. Clem Attlee Court, fronting Lillie Road, was built on a 10½ acre site in Fulham that had been badly bombed and also had a high proportion of substandard dwellings. The design of the three Y-shaped blocks, by Borough Architect J. Pritchard Lovell, was advanced for its time. The central staircase, two lifts and all services were accommodated in the centre of each block. A library was incorporated into the ground floor of one of these blocks and housing for the elderly was also provided at ground level. The estate was enlarged over the years and in 1974 an anthropologist, C. Leslie Andrews, lived for a year on the estate, which then housed 3,500 persons. Her report made depressing reading. Recently some of the blocks, including one of the Y-shaped blocks, have been demolished and new low-rise housing erected in its place. One of the roads has been named after John Smith, leader of the Labour Party, who died in 1994. The photograph below shows demolition work in progress in May 1997.

Poynter House, seen here during construction, *c.* 1967, was the first of the 24-storey tower blocks to be opened on the Edward Woods estate in the Latimer Road development area. The 15-acre development was named after Edward Woods, a former Mayor of Hammersmith who served on Hammersmith Borough Council for 40 years. Each of the 227 ft high tower blocks contained 176 flats with double-glazing, gas warm-air heating, a cabinet for drying clothes, a refrigerator and 'ample' cupboard space. Their namesake officially opened the flats on 16 March 1968.

All 'mod cons' in 1950 – a view of a spacious and up-to-date kitchen in a recently completed flat in Westville Road. A number of properties, including Westville Road School, had been destroyed during the Second World War on the night of 20/21 February 1944. A few days later the King and Queen visited several devastated bombsites in West London, including this one in Hammersmith. A new school, which was opened on 28 February 1952, and modern replacement flats were built after the war.

Flats at Brompton Park Crescent, shortly after completion in 1986. Brompton Park Crescent is a development of about 300 flats built by Barratt Central London Ltd 1984–6, and was one of the earliest in the country to provide its residents with their own private swimming pool and leisure complex. The flats were built on the site of the defunct Western Hospital, which had finally closed three years previously, and were arranged around 'two acres of open parkland'. The developers paid £5.4 million for the site and sold the completed properties for £46,500 to £84,000 with 999-year leases.

Chelsea Harbour and marina, 1991. Chelsea Harbour, a prestigious development built on a 20 acre triangle of derelict land once owned by British Rail, is bounded by the railway, Chelsea Creek and the river. The Creek, formerly part of the Kensington Canal, where herons can still sometimes be seen, is the boundary between Fulham and Chelsea. The scheme was the brainchild of architects Ray Moxley and Peter Bedford; construction began in 1986 and resulted in about 400 flats and houses plus parking for 2,000 cars. A special feature of the 'riverside village' community of about 3,000 residents and workers is the marina, formerly a derelict coal depot, which can accommodate about 60 yachts of up to 60 ft in length.

Chapter 3
Industry & Work

A view of the courtyard at Fulham Pottery in 1974. Founded in 1672 by John Dwight, the pottery was the first in England to successfully undertake the large-scale manufacture of salt-glaze stoneware. For nearly 300 years the pottery produced a wide range of goods including drinking vessels and bottles, storage containers, parts for water filters and decorative items for the home and garden. Many well-known potters and designers, including the Martin Brothers, C.I.C.Bailey and Constance Spry, worked at or had links with the pottery, which has now closed. In 1971 the Archaeological Section of the Fulham and Hammersmith Historical Society started excavations which revealed the locations of a number of kilns and produced large quantities of ceramic wares.

The borough's proximity to central London and its position on the river influenced its industrial development. Until the mid-19th century both Hammersmith and Fulham were predominantly rural, the main areas of employment being agriculture, particularly market gardening for the London markets; boat building, fishing, willow beds and other riverside occupations; and stables and forges on the western roads leading out of London. There was also industrial activity such as brickmaking, potteries and breweries. As the century progressed, improvements in public transport and the development of the locality with streets of houses provided new job opportunities.

Goods could be transported on the Thames, and the building of Hammersmith and Wandsworth Bridges encouraged industry. As a result three industrial zones and wharf developments had emerged by 1914, at Sands End, Crabtree and around Hammersmith Bridge and Creek. Most of the heavy industry was sited there, such as engineering, steel works, lead and oil mills and boat building. In Hammersmith these included Clark's Phoenix Lead Mills in Lower Mall, Gwynne's Iron Works in Crisp Road, Rosser and Russell's heating, ventilation and hydraulic engineering works at Queens Wharf, Vosper's boat building business at the Creek and Oil Mills in Upper Mall. The building firm of George Wimpey and Co. started in Hammersmith Grove in 1880. In Fulham the Anglo-American Oil Co. had established a wharf at Crabtree, later the Esso depot, by the turn of the century. A number of oil companies eventually had premises in Fulham, including the Shell-Mex BP depot and Total in Townmead Road, Petrofina in Carnwath Road and Duckham and Co. in Rainville Road. Several well-known car manufacturers were located in Seagrave Road, and Drayton Paper Works moved into Sulivan Road in 1913/14. But many other manufacturing or processing businesses in the borough were small, occupying cramped sites in residential areas.

A significant proportion of the borough's industries have been in the food and drink sector, with a special emphasis on sweet goods. The breweries that existed at the turn of the century have now closed. Stansfeld's (formerly the Swan Brewery), on a site occupied by Fulham Court, closed in 1928, and Kop's Brewery in Townmead Road became a margarine factory in about 1912, which itself closed in the early 1930s. Monsieur Manbré's factory, which manufactured a type of glucose called saccharine, came to Brandenburgh House Farm south of Hammersmith Bridge in 1873, and in 1926 it merged with Garton's to form Manbré & Garton. Until the late 1970s there was still a sugar refinery at the site, but it was demolished in 1979. J. Lyons and Co. made jam next door, and the idea was conceived of pumping the liquid glucose directly to its factory to speed up the jam-making process. Lyons' extensive main site was at Cadby Hall in Hammersmith Road, where it had bakeries, an ice-cream factory and offices, and it was a major local employer until it closed in the 1980s. Fuller's made cakes, chocolates and other sweet goods in Great Church Lane (now Talgarth Road) between 1900 and 1964. Macfarlane, Lang & Co. had a large biscuit factory in Townmead Road, which opened in 1903 but had closed by the 1930s. Other food factories included Telfer and Co. in Lillie Road, makers of sausage rolls and pork pies, the OK sauce factory in North End Road, the Vitamins factory which made Bemax, the House of Burgess in Hythe Road, some of whose goods were taken to the Antarctic by Captain Scott, and the quaintly named Findus Eskimo Frood factory in Rannoch Road.

The gas and power enterprises situated within the borough provided much employment in their heyday. In 1824 the Imperial Gas, Light and Coke Co. founded Fulham Gas Works on the Sandford Manor House site by Chelsea Creek. As late as the 1970s some 2,000 people were employed in the works and in the various adjacent Gas Board offices, but these have all closed now and the site is to be redeveloped. The No. 2 gas holder, built 1827–30, was the country's oldest working gas holder, and may survive because it is listed. Fulham Power Station was a municipal enterprise, built in 1901 after an electric lighting order was granted to Fulham Vestry in 1897. Before the Second World War it was served by a fleet of colliers owned and operated by Fulham Metropolitan Borough Council, all with the name 'Fulham'. The power station closed in 1978 and the site has been redeveloped. Until 1965 there was also a small power station in Hammersmith, just below Hammersmith Bridge. Other local businesses devoted to electricity included Osram and Robertson Lamp Co. (later part of GEC) and Julius Sax, who made electrical components.

From the mid-nineteenth century onwards the employment of women in Hammersmith and Fulham extended beyond domestic service and agriculture into factories, commercial laundries and every kind of industrial enterprise. From the turn of the century work of a less manual nature also became available for women, for example at the Post Office Savings Bank in Blythe Road, opened in 1903, which employed a high proportion of women, or at new enterprises such as the Lime Grove Studios, opened in 1913 as the first daylight film studio in the country and taken over by the BBC in 1950.

In the 1960s there were still some 400 factories in Hammersmith, especially in the north of the area, including a Rolls Royce factory in Hythe Road, but many have now closed. Further south the riverside industries in Hammersmith were effectively finished by both wartime bombing and the redevelopment of the riverside area. In Fulham, the unsuitability of the roads for large-scale road haulage has meant that the majority of big firms have moved away and their sites are now being developed for residential or mixed use. Occasionally there is a surviving reminder of the past, such as the restored bottle kiln in New King's Road which is all that remains of the famous Fulham Pottery, founded by John Dwight in about 1671 for the manufacture of stoneware, and closed in the 1990s. Today the main employers in the borough are the BBC, the local authority, service industries and offices. Office developments since the 1960s include the Empress State Building, the ICL premises by Putney Bridge, Hammersmith House in Queen Caroline Street and, more recently, the Bredero Centre West development at Hammersmith Broadway and the Ark in Talgarth Road. Many international companies, such as Seagram, Walt Disney, Coca-Cola, Polygram, HarperCollins and United International Pictures have chosen to site their headquarters in the borough.

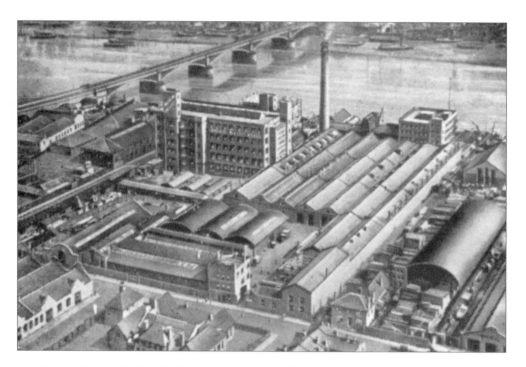

The origins of Macfarlane, Lang & Co. Ltd date back as far as 1817 when James Lang, a baker, opened premises in Gallowgate, Glasgow. On his death in 1841 the business was taken over by his nephew, John Macfarlane, who in turn took on his two elder sons, James and John, as partners in 1878. Subsequently the company decided to manufacture biscuits on a large scale using machinery, and the first baking was made in July 1886. At the same time the company's name was changed from John Macfarlane & Sons to Macfarlane, Lang & Co. Business boomed, necessitating frequent extensions to buildings and machinery. A depot was established in London in 1894, and as the extensions made to it soon proved inadequate, it was decided to build a factory in Townmead Road, Fulham, for the manufacture of biscuits for the London area and south of England. This opened in November 1903 and provided employment for over 1,000 men and women. Above, the aerial view of the site shows the works with Battersea Railway Bridge top left. Below, employees are sawing wafer sheets into finished shapes.

This view from the chimney of the first Fulham Power Station, Townmead Road, *c.* 1901, was taken looking towards the Lots Road Power Station, seen in the middle of the photograph. Within five years the land between the two power stations became built over as factories and other services moved to Fulham, providing much needed employment. Entries in the local street directory for 1903/4 show the presence on this site of Macfarlane, Lang & Co., biscuit manufacturers; John B. Lee & Sons, timber merchants; Wallington Jones & Co., refrigerator manufacturers and storage contractors; Mason, Scott & Co. Ltd, engineers and wheelwrights; and the Fulham Steel Works.

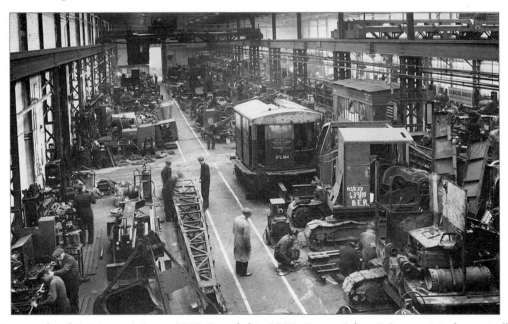

The Wood Lane works of T.C. Jones & Co., *c.* 1910. Founded in 1903, George Cohen & Sons acquired a controlling interest in the company in 1915. Cohen's, established in 1834 and trading in scrap metal, became one of the largest suppliers in the country of new, second-hand and reconditioned plant and machinery. The company broke up ships, and demolished the Great Wheel at Earls Court and also the Pimlico Gas Works. Over the years many companies were associated with Cohen's, which had become known as The '600' Group of Companies and by 1953/4 employed over 7,000 people. The company's name was an abbreviation of the head office address at 600 Commercial Road.

This photograph of Shingles Bakery at 90 Wandsworth Bridge Road was taken in about 1912, probably during the autumn months as the shop window has an advertisement on it advising that Christmas cakes can be made to order. The shop assistant on the left is holding a tabby kitten in her arms. At this date the business had two other branches, both in North End Road, and there were four other bakeries in Wandsworth Bridge Road. Mrs Charlotte Shingles, the owner of the business, was a widow living in Wimbledon.

Part of the production line for walnut cakes, *c.* 1909, at Fuller's factory in Great Church Lane, Hammersmith. William Bruce Fuller of Buffalo, USA, came to London in 1889 to exhibit peppermint lumps, fudge, coconut kisses and walnut cakes. Liking London, he stayed on and opened a shop selling these and similar delicacies. Six years later he had shops in Bayswater, Regent Street, Kensington and The Strand and a factory in Wardour Street. The factory was relocated to Hammersmith in 1900 and by the 1950s some 1,000 people were employed by the company. The valuable factory site was sold to Hammersmith Borough Council in 1964, and a year later the company had finally departed for Birmingham.

These two photographs show the cooperage at the Shell-Mex depot, *c.* 1920 (above) and women filling oilcans, possibly in the 1940s (below). Fulham's long river frontage has, over the years, provided employment for thousands as the site of many of the borough's industries, wharves and municipal undertakings such as the Fulham Power Station and refuse destructor. Biscuits, concrete, margarine, packing cases, iron, steel, lawnmowers, non-alcoholic beverages, pharmaceutical products, asphalt and tin boxes have all been manufactured there, while the wharves have provided facilities for the unloading and storage of goods such as slate, timber, cork, asbestos-cement sheets, stone and petroleum. Several oil companies were based

in Fulham, despite much initial opposition from the Council on safety grounds. British Petroleum and Shell-Mex, known as Shell-Mex BP from 1932, had several sites in Townmead Road. These all eventually closed down and the land was built over. When the closure of the last site was announced in 1983 it was said that 3,000 jobs had been lost in the Sands End area in the previous 10 years. Since the 1970s many other major industries have closed, consolidated or moved away from the Fulham river frontage to cheaper or more convenient locations.

Special vehicles carrying 14 tons of liquid sugar for Manbré & Garton Ltd, 1952. Manbré & Garton sugar refining company came to Fulham in the early 1870s. Its factory, completed in 1876, produced sugar from cereals, technically known as glucose, which was heavily used in the brewing industry. Other products included a cattle food made from maize, treacle, sugars for confectionery, preserves, ice cream, table jellies, baby foods, canned foods and liquid sugars. In 1931 it was realized that the latter could be pumped through from the refinery to the jam factory next door, saving time and money. The factory closed in the late 1970s and was demolished in 1978/9.

The attractive No. 3 gas holder at the Fulham Gas Works, c. 1969. The gas works, built on the Sandford Manor Estate, are among the oldest in the country and senior employees of the Imperial Gas Light & Coke Co. formerly occupied Sandford Manor House itself. The No. 2 holder was built in 1830 and is listed, while No. 3 was constructed some years later. In 1957 the works employed 850 men and produced 30 million cu. ft of gas a day. However, since natural gas from the North Sea began to be used in the 1970s, the site has become redundant. Plans for redeveloping 32 acres of the site have been put forward, with proposals for 900 homes, shops, hotel and leisure facilities.

Unemployed men advertise a boxing tournament at the Hammersmith Baths in Lime Grove, December 1920, which raised £104 for the Mayor of Hammersmith's Unemployment Fund. The First World War was followed by unemployment, and efforts were made to alleviate the hardships suffered by the jobless. In Hammersmith an Unemployment Committee, consisting of representatives of the Council, employers, ex-servicemen, labour organizations and civilian unemployed, was set up and held its first meeting on 11 November 1920. Schemes were devised that provided employment through essential work such as road building.

The British Industries Fair, 1936. First held in 1921, the Fair provided an important shop window for buyers from home and abroad. From 1921 to 1937 they took place at the White City. The first British Cotton Exhibition was held in 1931 at Olympia, and from 1932 to 1937 both events were spread between the two sites, after which they moved to Olympia and Earls Court. The King and Queen were regular visitors to the exhibitions, which showed goods ranging from furniture to fabrics, electrical goods to toys and photographic equipment to boots and shoes.

Construction work in progress on the Wormholt estate, *c.* 1920. This estate was built on 125 acres of land acquired by Hammersmith Borough Council from the Ecclesiastical Commissioners in 1919 for £74,165. The houses, built initially for ex-servicemen and for sale to local residents, were designed by a panel of five 'eminent' architects including R. Hampton Clucas, the Borough Engineer and Surveyor, and Henry T. Hare. The latter, formerly President of the RIBA, had also designed Hammersmith Central Library and Fulham Central Library. The estate was described as 'a most desirable residential locality, with excellent facilities for travelling by rail or road to all parts of London'.

Workmen from the coal depot next to the London & South Western Railway's Hammersmith (The Grove) station, early 1900s. It is not known why this photograph was taken, but as the gentleman on the left has an accordion it may be a lunch break. The station, on the Kensington & Richmond Railway of the LSWR, was opened on 1 January 1869 and closed in June 1916. The line came from Richmond and crossed over The Grove (later Hammersmith Grove), looped round to the northern end of Shepherds Bush Road and then down to Kensington (Addison Road) Station. Twenty years after closure the station was demolished and the bridge, seen in the background, was removed in 1956.

The ironing room at the Sunlight Laundry,
Broughton Road, Fulham, 1939, and a cartoon
relating to the Whitewash Laundry, Munster Road,
c. 1912. Judging by the number of entries in local
street directories, parts of Fulham must have smelt
permanently of soapsuds. There were large
laundries belonging to Messrs William Whiteley
near the present-day junction of North End Road
and the West Cromwell Road, the Carnwath
Laundry, Fulham Imperial Laundry, the Walham
Green Henrici Laundry and the Sunlight Laundry.
There was also a large number of smaller
establishments such as the Whitewash Laundry.
The Sunlight Laundry in Broughton Road had in
1900 a ground space of over 12,000 sq. ft on one
floor. Laundry was delivered by van and on arrival
it was sorted and checked before being taken to
the granite and cement floored washhouse. After
washing and water extraction, the laundry was
taken to drying rooms and in due course ironed
and aired before being packed for return to the
customer. The laundry had a number of receiving
offices in London including several in Fulham.

The new headquarters of the Post Office Savings Bank in Blythe Road, which opened in 1903, cost £270,000 to build and a further £45,000 for the site. Building operations took nearly four years. The bank, designed by Henry Tanner, was believed to be the largest savings bank in the world, accommodating 4,000 persons and with provision to take on another 3,000. At the time of opening, over 3,000 clerks were employed, of which nearly half were women. Three refreshment rooms were provided – two for women and one for men. One of them is pictured above, *c.* 1903. Other facilities included electric lighting, five lifts and 'every modern comfort and convenience'. In 1903 the bank had over 9 million account holders, who made 15 million deposits and 6 million withdrawals through 14,000 post office banks. All these transactions were dealt with and recorded at the new building, where a daily average of 100,000 letters was received. As can be seen from the photograph below, *c.* 1952, showing some of the clerks at work, a very high proportion of them were women. In the late 1970s the National Savings Bank, as it was then known, closed and moved to 'more sophisticated premises' and the building now houses the archives of the Victoria & Albert Museum.

The morning parade at Hammersmith police station, 1950s. The parade was held 15 minutes before the start of duties and was conducted by either the superintendent or sergeant. The purpose of the parade was to brief officers on crimes that had been perpetrated, other matters such as empty properties and faulty traffic lights, to pass on messages and assign them to their patrols for the day. Officers were not paid for this time, during which their uniforms were also inspected to ensure that they were clean and smart, and their 'appointments', consisting of truncheon, whistle and notebooks, were checked. Today the parade is rather more informal.

A rag and bone man in the Latimer Road area, late 1960s. Recycling is not a modern phenomenon although people are now much more aware of the need to save metals, paper and glass for re-use. The rag and bone man, epitomized by the BBC TV series *Steptoe and Son*, still plays an important part in the process of collecting unwanted items for recycling. In the 1950s it was common for children to collect unwanted newspapers from local householders and take them, usually in an old pram or pushchair, to a scrap dealer who would weigh them and pay a small sum for each pound of paper delivered to him. This was a useful supplement to one's pocket money.

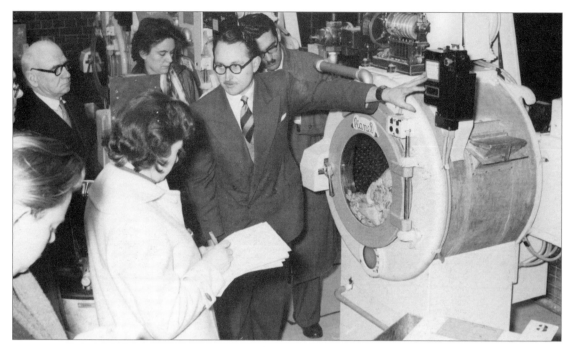

All in a day's work as the Hammersmith Baths Superintendent, H.T. Hitchin, demonstrates the new washing machines at the Lime Grove Baths in January 1957, when this first automated public laundry in the country came into operation. The machines cost 2s 6d (12½p) and in one hour 24 lb of laundry could be washed and dried, while provision was also made for ironing. In most other public washhouses this task could take 2½ hours. The laundry needed only one supervisor, but reductions of staff had been made without the need for redundancies. Existing staff were expected to earn more for doing a more responsible job.

William Luff's violin workshop in Wood Lane was described in 1955, when this photograph was taken, as 'like stepping into a bygone age'. Mr Luff started to play the violin in 1920 but an injury to his left hand interrupted his studies, so he decided to learn to make and repair violins instead, studying under Maximillian Milant in Paris. In a period of 35 years he repaired 12,000 violins, cellos and basses using seasoned woods, rare varnishes, maple chippings, resin, catgut and horsehair. He also made many instruments and came into contact with some of the world's finest players. The photograph shows Mr Luff with a bridge that he had carved for the bass he is holding.

Chapter 4
Trade & Shopping

This photograph of a fish stall formed part of the Clean Food Exhibition at the Borough of Fulham's Golden Jubilee Civic Exhibition at the public baths in North End Road, 28 October to 4 November 1950. The Medical Officer of Health's department in Fulham had a duty to see that foods were of an acceptable standard of cleanliness and purity, and prosecutions could be brought if hygiene regulations were flouted. The stall was fitted with a refrigerator powered by a generator, to keep the fish cool, and with special transparent display cases to keep flies and dust away.

By the early years of this century, building development and the growth in population had attracted many small shops to the main streets of Hammersmith and Fulham and to terraces situated in residential streets. There were also a few larger drapers' establishments, and the occasional department store. Walham Green was the main shopping centre in Fulham, and King Street in Hammersmith. Shop opening hours were long, often until 11.00 p.m. on a weekday night and later on Saturdays, and shop work or even proprietorship of a shop was a useful employment option for women who needed to earn a living. Goods, including perishable foodstuffs such as meat, were sometimes displayed outside the shops, and small dairy farms such as Glover's Dairy Farm at 15 Brook Green Road and Vicarage Dairy Farm at 796 Fulham Road still provided fresh milk and dairy products. Milk was sold from the churn on floats and other goods were sold on the streets in barrows, although the practice of street selling from baskets and on pavements was dying out.

The larger establishments included Barbers and Timothy Davies in Fulham and Palmers in Hammersmith. Timothy Davies, who opened his draper's shop at Fulham Broadway in 1885, later became Mayor of Fulham in 1901/2 and its MP between 1906 and 1910. By the 1930s the shop was a household goods department store, occupying 30,000 sq. ft, but it was sold during the Second World War. F.H. Barber, who founded Barber's in North End Road, also became Mayor of Fulham. His shop, which opened in 1891, eventually occupied a whole block and did not close until the 1990s. Palmers was at the junction of King Street and Hammersmith Broadway, a family business selling food, clothing, household furnishings and china and glass. It closed in 1953 and the site has now been redeveloped. Some local manufacturing businesses had trade connections both locally and in London. Chibnall's Bakery, which started in Chiswick Mall in 1887, had several bakery shop outlets, including one in King Street, while L.E. Jolly Ltd, which began business as a cooked meat and pie manufacturers at 24 King Street in 1910, had 24 retail branches throughout London by the 1960s. Shops sometimes lent their names to road junctions, such as Poppy's Corner at the junction of Lillie Road and North End Road, named after A.W. Poppy's ladies' outfitter's store, which existed there between about 1900 and 1924. Gapp's grocer's shop was situated opposite, and later the junction became known as Gapp's Corner. An unusual shop was the Metropolitan Borough of Fulham's Electricity Department showroom at 603 Fulham Road, opened in 1911, where lighting and heating appliances could be obtained, and cookers hired.

North End Road Market is thought to have been established in the 1880s when costers migrated there from the western end of Kings Road. Although the stalls obstruct traffic in the road, the market shows no signs of dying. Hammersmith Market, which survives in a very limited form, is at least a century old. It moved into Bradmore Lane in 1906 and then into Hammersmith Grove in the 1970s, following the King's Mall development. It sold mainly fruit, vegetables, fish and flowers. Shepherds Bush Market was opened in 1914 in what had formerly been the access road to the old Shepherds Bush Metropolitan Line station, replaced in the same year by two new stations in Goldhawk Road and Uxbridge Road. There were already shops in the railway arches, and the shopkeepers were far from pleased when costers were allowed to set up their barrows in competition, objecting also to their loud shouting and the smell of fish from the fish stalls. In fact street markets can bring extra trade to shops situated behind the stalls, as they attract more shoppers into the street. Shepherds Bush Market closed during the First World War and was bombed during the Second World War, but survived and still flourishes. In the 1970s the market had many Arab customers, who appreciated its bazaar atmosphere.

In the decades since the Second World War the pattern of shopping has changed. The effects of wartime bombing and changes in working practices meant that small shops were not well placed to withstand competition from the new supermarkets which opened from the 1950s onwards and have now grown to such an extent that they have forced many smaller shops, such as greengrocers and butchers, out of business. The Lyons supermarket in Hammersmith Road, opened in February 1956 and at that time the largest in west London, was a well-known early supermarket in this area. Some supermarkets have been built on land vacated when industries departed the borough, such as Sainsbury's on the former Fulham Power Station site at Sands End. Chain stores have tended to replace the local drapers' shops, chemists, bookshops, shoe shops, opticians, stationers and similar businesses. At present the borough is not particularly well served by clothes shops or department stores, perhaps because of competition from neighbouring retail areas such as Kensington High Street and Putney. Opening hours have increased again, reflecting the fact that both men and women now work and have little time during the day to shop. In Fulham many expensive antique, furniture, and interior decoration shops have opened to cater for the well-off people who are buying homes in the area. Since the 1970s covered shopping malls and centres, such as King's Mall in King Street, opened in 1979, the Hammersmith Broadway Shopping Centre, opened in the early 1990s, and the proposed development at the White City, have been popular with town planners.

Vicarage Farm Dairy at 796 Fulham Road, *c.* 1905. The name 'Holcroft's Pavement' can be partially seen just above the shop blind on the right of the photograph. Holcroft's was the name of a large house which stood on the corner of Fulham Road and Fulham Palace Road and gave its name to the properties that were built on part of the site after it was demolished in 1887. Milk was sold from the churn on the float, using the measuring jugs seen on the side. Thomas Ball had his dairy at this address 1892–1907.

For those who could afford it, a visit to Oliver Rowe's shop at 7 Colehill Lane in about 1910 would ensure that their feet were comfortable in hand-stitched shoes made from the best English leather. The business had several branches in New Kings Road, Fulham Road, Lillie Road, Vanston Place and Broughton Road Approach. For the less well-off, Rowe's could provide a repair service which included the fitting of new soles and revolving heels. The latter could be turned as the edge became worn down and thus extend the life of the owner's shoes.

This photograph of the premises of Farmer James Bates, 'the noted labouring mans butcher' at 115 Askew Road, *c.* 1904, does not inspire confidence about the hygiene of the meat on display. The photograph may have been taken near Christmas as there are bunches of leaves, perhaps holly, decorating the carcasses of meat. The weather would have been cooler and the risk of contamination from flies, but not dust, rather less. The business was established in 1880 and at one time there was another shop at 112 Askew Road, almost opposite. On the left of the photograph is James Bates with his wife Ellen, and his eldest son, also James, is on the chair in the middle.

The newspaper shop of Arthur E. Prentice, 295 New Kings Road, October 1911. The window of this shop is a real Aladdin's cave with displays of fireworks, costing 1s per dozen, picture postcards and a wonderful collection of newspaper headlines. The headlines 'How fight for a throne failed' and 'Panic at Peking' relate to the anti-Manchu revolution in China and 'Driven out of Tripoli' to the Turco-Italian War. The *Illustrated London News* of the time published disturbing photographs of both wars, including an execution by firing squad and the decapitated heads of Chinese rebels. It is unclear what the 'Adventures of Sulky Sue' were!

A.E. West's domestic stores at 140 Goldhawk Road, *c.* 1910, with a wonderful jumble of bowls, rugs, clothes-horses, teapots, ladders, ewers, coal scuttles, ladders, watering cans and washing bowls juxtaposed with the open-air display of meat at the butcher's shop next door. The domestic stores also sold lamps, saucepans, kerosene and watches. One wonders how long it took to arrange the goods and what happened when it rained. Stores such as this are rarely seen today even in country towns and villages.

The greengrocer's shop of Henry Edward Stow at 3–5 Vanston Place, Fulham, *c.* 1914. John Pitman, one of the employees, is in the centre wearing a barely discernible striped tie. Mr Rabson is the cart-driver and he is holding a little girl, Miss Stone, on his lap. The shop was originally located at 9-11 Vanston Place but had to move when the Red Hall Picture Palace, which opened in December 1913, was constructed on its site. The display of fruit and vegetables seems to have taken over the temporarily vacant site of no. 7, between Stow's and the new cinema.

A busy scene in the market in North End Road, *c.* 1904. The market, which runs between Lillie Road and Walham Grove, is thought to have spread north up the North End Road in the 1880s, when costers migrated there from the western end of Kings Road. It was well known for its fruit and vegetable stalls and lively characters, and attracted visitors from all over London. Over the years there have been a number of unsuccessful plans to move the market because of traffic congestion. Today, although the market continues to sell its traditional goods, a wide range of other items is available including rugs, toiletries, household items and CDs.

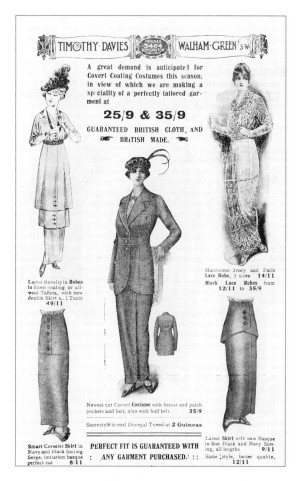

Timothy Davies, Fulham's second mayor in 1901/2, had opened a tiny draper's shop in Fulham Broadway in 1885. The business prospered and within 50 years had expanded from a store with a selling area of 540 sq. ft to 30,000 sq. ft, becoming one of the largest ground-floor stores in London. This meant that there were 'no wearying stairs to climb' to reach the various departments, which included furniture, china and glass, millinery, underclothing, outerwear, drapery, shoes, carpets, linoleum and general household goods. A yard and stabling were acquired for the horses and carts which delivered goods. Davies was in advance of his time and had installed an electric light plant at the store before the Council had built its own power station. For many years his were the only premises in Fulham lit by electricity. The Second World War brought changes; the shop was sold and then allowed to stand empty for several years, becoming rather derelict. The upper part was purchased by the Council for conversion into flats, and the lower part became offices. The top illustration is from the 'Autumn Fashions' catalogue of 1914; below is the store, *c.* 1910.

The after-effects of the Second World War can clearly be seen in this photograph of Messrs Lyons' Staff Stores in Hammersmith Road, 1949. The stores were opened for the company's employees after the war and closed in 1956 when a new supermarket also run by Lyons, the largest in west London, was built in its place, opening on 13 February 1956. This too closed when Cadby Hall, the Lyons works site, was demolished in 1983. In the years of food rationing after the war 'points' had to be exchanged for each of certain items, mainly staples such as meat, tea, sugar, butter, eggs. The cans of steak and kidney puddings seen at the back of the store cost 1s 3d (8p) and 4 points.

Hammersmith Market, 13 April 1972. This market, whose exact origins are unknown but date back well over 100 years, was originally located in King Street but moved into Bradmore Lane in 1906. At the end of 1972 it moved to a temporary site a little to the east when the land was required for the Kings Mall development, which included a shopping centre, offices, car parking, some housing and the new Lyric Theatre. A further move to its present site, in Hammersmith Grove, followed several years later. The market sold mainly fruit, vegetables, fish, some household goods and flowers. Today it is a shadow of its former self.

'Uncle Albert' in Shepherds Bush Market, 1953, dealing out toffee apples to George Kenter and Raymond Lascelles. Shepherds Bush Market, one of London's best known, was formally opened on 3 July 1914, although it had been in existence for some years before then. It is situated in the old access road to Shepherds Bush Metropolitan Line Station, which closed in 1914 when two replacement stations, Goldhawk Road and Shepherds Bush, were built at either end of the market. The old booking office became the market office. The market has always been popular, especially with sweet-toothed youngsters and those looking for a bargain.

The Tesco supermarket at 134 King Street, Hammersmith, opened on 12 April 1961 and was 'equipped for modern shopping'. The store was built in the converted Windsor Castle public house and provided 3,400 sq. ft of floor space where fresh meat and vegetables 'direct from our packing station at Covent Garden' could be purchased in addition to the usual range of foods and household goods. Over 4,000 lines of proprietary foods were advertised as being sold at permanently cut prices. Friday night was designated as a family shopping night when the store stayed open until 7.30 p.m. This photograph was taken in 1961 shortly after the store had opened.

Chapter 5
People & Their Lives

Your life would be revolutionized if you purchased this gadget from Mr Alfred Mordeia in Shepherds Bush Market, seen here in 1953. The gadget in question was an eggbeater that could transform an egg white and its yolk into an enormous omelette. Mr Mordeia would whisk the egg white in a tumbler until thick and solid, add the egg yolk and cook it in front of a large audience. The addition of sugar made it especially interesting to the children who gathered to watch, as when it was finished the omelette would be cut into pieces and offered around. No doubt this would contravene all health and hygiene regulations today.

Most of the photographs in this book show the built environment in Hammersmith and Fulham, but the life of a place is in its people. The photographs in this chapter have been chosen to show ordinary people living and working in the borough. Fashions and the local scene may change, but human nature does not.

Modern London is a cosmopolitan city, and this borough is no exception. There has been a lively mix of people in the area for at least two centuries, due to a number of factors: the varied social make-up of Hammersmith and Fulham; the existence until recently of large numbers of industries and businesses; the presence in the borough of important institutions such as a bishop's palace, three professional football clubs, Olympia, Wormwood Scrubs Prison, two large hospitals and BBC Television Centre; and the arrival of ethnic communities in significant numbers. Local people have never been insular, based as they are on the river and on two major western routes into London. Perhaps this has enabled them to cope better with the great changes which have taken place in the borough since the Second World War, as demolition and reconstruction of buildings and roads have happened all around them.

The borough has been enriched by the different ethnic communities which have settled here. Perhaps the oldest established is the Irish community. The Irish arrived mainly from the 1830s onwards, when a curate taking up his post in Fulham found 'a pretty village, approached through market gardens and, except for a colony of Irish (who are frozen out every winter), inhabited by well-to-do people'. They settled in the Fulham Fields and Walham Green areas, inhabiting houses which were overcrowded and badly built, and around Brook Green and central Hammersmith, where there were eventually so many Catholic institutions that it was known as Pope's Corner. The Hammersmith parish records for 1837 note 'a great increase of poor Irish at Brook Green and other parts of the Parish, who at times literally besiege the workhouse'. The 1851 census records 1,685 people in the area who were born in Ireland, 5.7 per cent of the population. In the mid-19th century they worked mostly in the local market gardens and as general labourers, servants and laundresses, and later on as railway workers and building labourers during the building boom of the late 19th century. Churches such as St Thomas', Rylston Road (1847–9), and St Augustine's, Fulham Palace Road (1915–16) were built to serve the Irish community. Michael Collins, the famous Irish nationalist, soldier and politician, lived in Netherwood Road, W14, 1914–15, and worked as a clerk at the Post Office Savings Bank in Blythe Road. There was another period of increased immigration from Ireland after the Second World War, when workers were needed for post-war reconstruction. The 1991 census records 12,690 people living in borough households whose heads were born in Ireland, some 9 per cent of the local population, and they are still the largest ethnic minority group resident in the borough. A number of organizations were started by and for Irish people, including the Hibernian Club, the Emerald Centre and the Irish Centre, and services such as the Irish Support and Advice Service. Nowadays the largest concentration of Irish people is in the Shepherds Bush area, in some other parts of Hammersmith and on the White City estate.

There is also a substantial Polish community in west London. Hitler's invasion of Poland on 1 September 1939 marked the outbreak of the Second World War, and after the war many Polish people who had come here as servicemen, and a few as refugees, chose to stay on. The Presbyterian Church of St Andrew in Leysfield Road, Shepherds Bush, was bought in 1961 to serve the Polish community and rededicated to St Andrew Bobola, a seventeenth-century Polish martyr, and the Polish Cultural and Social Centre in King Street was opened in 1974. The 1991 census data shows that 18 per cent of the borough's population falls within ethnic groups other than 'white', compared with 26 per cent in Inner London and 6 per cent in England and Wales as a whole. Some 8,820 people, or 6 per cent of the local population, are black Caribbeans, mainly as a result of the increase in immigration from the Caribbean to London in the 1950s and 1960s when London Transport and other enterprises needed workers. Among the most eminent local black people are the runner Linford Christie, who was brought up and educated in the borough, and Randolph Beresford, trade unionist and the first black Mayor of the borough. Other black groups, including black Africans, account for some 5 per cent of the borough's population, as do Asians, including Indians, Pakistanis, Bangladeshis and Chinese. The Indian community arrived mainly in the post-war period, and in the 1970s from East Africa, the Pakistanis and Bangladeshis arrived in the 1960s and 1970s, and the Chinese community mostly originates from Hong Kong, Vietnam and other parts of south-east Asia. Greek and Turkish Cypriots are also represented. But these statistics are only part of the story. The Hammersmith and Fulham Libraries' database of community organizations reveals the sheer number of different nationalities represented in the borough, including people who unfortunately are forced to be refugees from their own countries. The borough is privileged to experience such cultural and racial diversity in its daily life, reflected by the 80 or more languages spoken by people in Hammersmith and Fulham.

The greengrocer and fruiterer's shop of C. Ade at 50 New Kings Road, Fulham, *c.* 1904. At this time Mrs Caroline Ade ran her own business, which obviously attracted a wide clientele. The produce she sold may have come from one of Fulham's market gardens. She is rated for the premises, which was very close to Parsons Green, from October 1896 to 17 November 1910. The adjacent properties were destroyed during the Second World War, and the site remained vacant for many years until rebuilding took place in about 1997.

The Snowdrop Laundry van in North End Road, *c.* 1914. Before the days of launderettes and domestic washing machines, laundry was done at home using a 'copper' to boil the water, or was entrusted to a laundrywoman or taken to one of the laundries run by the local authority or a private company. One popular and inexpensive scheme, particularly for large families, was the 'bagwash', whereby the contents of a cotton bag, usually sheets, pillow cases, shirts, handkerchiefs etc., could be laundered ready for ironing and final drying. A similar scheme was available for oily overalls. The Snowdrop Laundry at 100 Greyhound Road, one of many laundries in Fulham, made daily collections in the area using a horse-drawn van.

Above and right: The tailoring shop at Wormwood Scrubs Prison, *c.* 1895, and prisoners waiting to be served lunch, 1956. The prison was built by its inmates between 1874 and 1891 to the designs of Maj.-Gen. Edmund Frederick Du Cane, the Chairman of the Directors of Convict Prisons. In 1895 there were separate cells for 1,381 prisoners, plus hospital accommodation for 50 men and 29 women which included a lying-in ward with four beds. Women were housed at the prison 1891–1902. Prisoners wore uniforms relating to their 'status' within the prison and many were employed in the making of mailbags, mats, coal sacks etc. in their cells, while others did tailoring, carpentry, shoemaking and bookbinding. In 1894 the prisoners made 142,000 mailbags and the value of labour performed by them amounted to £20,509. The 1956 photograph shows row upon row of grim iron doors in one of the cellblocks. The 'suicide' net can clearly be seen between the landings under which the prisoners are standing.

Police Specials parading outside Craven Cottage for football duty, 1951. The match was between the reserve teams of Fulham Football Club and West Ham United in the Combination Cup on 27 January 1951, and the result was a 0–0 draw. Police Specials, all unpaid volunteers, are still called on to attend events where large numbers of people are expected to gather, to assist the local police in providing security and crowd control.

Children from St Matthew's parish, Fulham, *c.* 1900. The photograph was made from a lantern slide, one of a series taken to show daily life in the Sands End area. Here the children can be seen carrying milk pails and jugs and they appear to be watching another photographer whose camera tripod legs can be seen on the right. Other views in the series include women working in the fields, the Church Lads Brigade at camp, workers at Kops Brewery, St Matthew's Church, and a clergyman visiting parishioners. St Matthew's, on the corner of Wandsworth Bridge Road and Rosebury Road, which was consecrated in April 1895, was demolished in early 1999. Rebuilding is expected to finish in time for the Millennium.

Employees of the Manbré saccharine company leaving the works in Winslow Road to join the national protest against the Licensing Bill in Hyde Park on Sunday 27 September 1908. The 18,000 London marchers were made up of about 10,000 men from the London brewery companies, 4,500 from the allied trades and many independent protesters, and they joined a 2-mile long procession. Over 1,000 of them were from Fulham. Thirty bands provided music for the marchers. The protest against the bill was 'on the grounds that it will fail to promote the cause of temperance, will tend largely to the increase of unemployment and will interfere with the reasonable liberty of the community'.

Another character from Shepherds Bush Market, doing his best to brighten a dull day in 1953, was 'Lucky' King, king of banjo players, seen here with two young admirers. Author Christine Bayliss remembers that the market was a haven for children. One special attraction was the pet shop where one could touch the rabbits, kittens and puppies in their cages and look at the brightly coloured budgerigars and other singing birds. This shop had its own special smell. The sweet stalls too were always of interest, especially the one that sold great lumps of cough candy twist and other boiled sweets; and, if all else failed, it was amusing to listen to the patter of the china and pottery salesman or the 'medicine man'.

The self-styled 'Gypsy Queen', Margaret Barry, at the first gathering of Irish traditional musicians at the Hibernian Centre, Fulham, late 1950s. The borough has had a large Irish community since the nineteenth century, and the Hibernian was a very important centre for them and for Irish music. Margaret Barry, an Irish traveller by origin, was an important figure in the traditional music world in the 1950s and thus had a big influence on Irish balladeers in the 1960s. Prior to 1955 the building occupied by the Hibernian Centre, tucked behind Fulham Broadway Station, had been a cinema.

About 1,000 'long-haired boys and girls in hippy dress' attended this free open-air pop concert on Wormwood Scrubs, 22 August 1970. The concert started two hours late and coincided with the first of several downpours of rain. Some of the audience sheltered under the scaffolding holding up the stage and others huddled together under umbrellas, towels and polythene sheets. The braver ones just stood in the open and got wet. Near the end of the concert, which was curtailed at 6 p.m., some skinheads arrived looking for trouble but the police presence ensured that there was none. Quintessence, the top of the bill group, did not even have time to play.

The demolition of Fulham Power Station, Townmead Road, 16 May 1985. The power station was built in 1936 by Fulham Borough Council and at the time of its construction it was the largest power station in municipal ownership in the country. In 1948 it was transferred to the British Electricity Authority, and converted to oil in 1972. Six years later it became obsolete. The property was sold in 1983 and demolition and preparation for asbestos stripping began almost immediately. Local residents were very concerned about the asbestos risks and work was stopped for a time to enable safety measures to be implemented. Demolition was finally completed about three years later. The exclusive Harbour Club now occupies the site.

Two high-level views of Hammersmith. The top view, taken in 1996, is of 'The Ark', a modern office block designed by Ralph Erskine for a Swedish construction company, Ake Larsen, as its European headquarters. The block was built on the site of the old Metropolitan Police car pound. Work on the distinctive and controversial nine-storey block, built around a dramatic central atrium, began late in 1989 and was completed in 1992. However, owing to a recession in the property market it was not until 1996 that an occupier, Seagram Co. Ltd, was found. The 'crow's nest' at the top of the building provides a wonderful aerial view of this part of west London. The lower photograph was taken in 1973 and shows how much this part of Hammersmith has changed in 25 years. St Paul's Church can be seen on its island-like site, surrounded by busy roads, while on the far right is the recently completed Charing Cross Hospital. To the left of the church is Hammersmith Broadway, now completely demolished and rebuilt. Behind this and towards the top of the picture is the first of several new office blocks and the new Cunard Hotel (now the Novotel) under construction. The Ark has yet to be built near the point at which Hammersmith Flyover returns to ground level.

A power cut affected one of the two performances of a Nativity play at Canberra School, on the White City estate, in December 1970. The power cut meant that the children's parents could not hear recordings of carols but 'in true show-business tradition the show had to go on'. Mrs Newbold made the costumes and the school's Deputy Headmistress, Miss Beatrice Bartley, produced the play. The part of Joseph was played by John Hunt and the three kings by Paul Inboll, Perry Wood and Thomas Aimable.

Albert Betts, the chef, with children at teatime at the Rylston Road Day Nursery, 1978. Albert's cakes were great favourites with the children and he made special cakes to celebrate birthdays. In 1978 the London Borough of Hammersmith and Fulham had 9 day nurseries, each with about 50 places for children. Each nursery employed a cook, cleaners, kitchen and laundry staff as well as having a matron-in-charge and professional staff. Between them they cared for children whose ages ranged from new born to five years.

Chapter 6
Faith & Education

This certificate was awarded to Leonard Bayliss, a pupil at Munster Road School, in 1917. Many people looking at old photographs showing classroom scenes or posed groups of schoolchildren will have noticed a number of pupils wearing medals. These were awarded by the School Board for London and later the LCC for attendance and punctuality. Some pupils won as many as eight of these. Prizes were also awarded for educational achievements. During the First World War the award of medals and prizes was suspended and certificates issued instead, which must have disappointed many pupils.

The most significant development in education before this century was Forster's Education Act of 1870, which introduced state education. Prior to the Act, education was provided either by the Anglican Church and Nonconformist churches through the National Schools and British Schools, or by charities, or privately. Some local schools have been in existence for centuries, evolving through the various changes and new legislation which have affected education in this country.

Many of the schools in the borough were originally church schools, such as All Saints School now in Bishops Avenue, which was probably founded in 1610 and became a National School in the 19th century, and St John's, Fulham Broadway, built in 1836, which moved to the former Munster School site in 1997. The School Board for London, which was set up after the Education Act of 1870, had an ambitious programme of building schools and had built 26 in Fulham alone by the time it was abolished in 1902. The London County Council (LCC) took over from the School Board in 1904 and built new secondary schools, while some of the Board schools were developed into central schools, which specialized in technical and commercial training for children who had not gone to grammar school. In 1965 the Inner London Education Authority assumed the management of schools, until it was abolished in its turn in 1986 and boroughs such as Hammersmith and Fulham became Local Education Authorities in their own right. Non-selective comprehensive schools were introduced in 1965. Because of changing views of education and resulting legislation, and of other factors such as wartime bombing, many schools in the borough have moved, amalgamated and changed names. For example, the name of Burlington Danes School, now a comprehensive, reflects the fact that it was an amalgamation of two former schools: St Clement Danes Grammar School for Boys, which opened in 1862, moved to Hammersmith in 1928, and relocated again to Hertfordshire in 1976 apart from its local pupils, and The Burlington School (for girls), founded in 1699 and relocated from St James, Westminster, to Wood Lane in 1936. Hammersmith County School in White City recently changed its name to Phoenix School as part of an initiative to improve the school and its image.

The borough is known for its ancient and well-respected private schools, some of which moved to this area from central London when they needed to expand and were looking for cheaper, healthier sites in less urban locations. Latymer Upper School evolved from the Latymer Foundation School, a charitable foundation school dating from 1624, and opened on its present site in King Street in 1895. St Paul's School came to Hammersmith in 1884 from the City, but moved out of the borough to Barnes in 1968. The school buildings in Hammersmith Road, which were built by Alfred Waterhouse, were demolished in 1970 except for the High Master's house. St Paul's Girls' School in Brook Green opened in 1904, and Godolphin and Latymer Girls' School, in Iffley Road, in 1906. The music department of St Paul's Girls' School can boast of two celebrated past music masters, Gustav Holst and Herbert Howells. Holst, who became Musical Director in 1905, had already lived in Hammersmith for some years and conducted the choir of William Morris' Hammersmith Socialist Society. He wrote 'The Planets', 'Hammersmith Suite' and 'Brook Green Suite' while teaching at St Paul's, and continued working there until his death in 1934.

Schools in the borough continue to evolve, partly as a result of legislation in the 1980s and '90s which has allowed schools greater freedom to manage themselves. Many local pupils now take their 'A' levels at the William Morris Academy in St Dunstan's Road, opened in 1994. Church schools remain among the best in the borough, and include Lady Margaret School, Parsons Green, which was founded in about 1917 by Enid Moberley Bell and named after Lady Margaret Tudor, mother of Henry VII. The Prime Minister, Tony Blair (whose election mantra was 'Education, education, education') has chosen to send two of his children to Roman Catholic schools in the borough: Sacred Heart High School (established 1893), in Hammersmith Road, and the Oratory School in Seagrave Road, which moved to Fulham from Chelsea in 1970.

Between about 1830 and 1930, some 23 new Anglican churches were built in Hammersmith and Fulham to cater for the rapidly expanding population, and there was a similar growth in Catholic and Nonconformist places of worship. Several Roman Catholic churches in the borough were built after the turn of the century: St Augustine's, Fulham Palace Road, opened 1916, Our Lady of Perpetual Succour, Stephendale Road, 1922, and the Church of the Holy Cross, Ashington Road, 1924. However, Anglican church attendance had reached a peak in the late 19th century, and by 1900 had already started to fall. The problem of declining congregations has been solved in recent years by closing and demolishing churches and amalgamating parishes, a process accelerated by the bomb damage of the Second World War, which enabled several churches to be rebuilt in smaller, more modern form. St Mary's, West Kensington, St Etheldreda's, Fulham Palace Road, and St Catherine's, Primula Street, were all destroyed by bombs and rebuilt, as were Askew Road Methodist Church and Uxbridge Road Tabernacle. Other places of worship have disappeared altogether, including St Clement's, demolished in 1969, St Oswald's, Ongar Road, demolished in 1977, Oaklands Congregational Church, a handsome neo-classical building demolished in the 1980s, and St James', Moore Park Road, which burnt down shortly after it had been made redundant. Some churches have been remodelled internally to make them more up to date, such as St John's, Walham Green, and St Peter's, Varna Road, another bomb-damaged church, while one or two churches have been built since the war, such as St Michael and St George, consecrated in 1953, and Our Lady of Fatima, completed in about 1965, both on the White City estate.

The different ethnic communities which now reside in the borough have left their mark on its religious life, and local places of worship include the New Testament Church of God, Redmore Road, the Hungarian Reformed Church in St Dunstan's Road, the Muslim Mosque in Uxbridge Road and the West Kensington and Hammersmith Synagogue at Brook Green. The former Presbyterian Church of St Andrew has been rededicated to St Andrew Bobola, a seventeenth-century Polish martyr, to serve the Polish community in Hammersmith, and the West Kensington Congregational Church in Challoner Street, built in 1885 by James Cubitt and sometimes visited by Mahatma Gandhi when he was a student, is now the Bharat Vidya Bhavan Indian Cultural Centre.

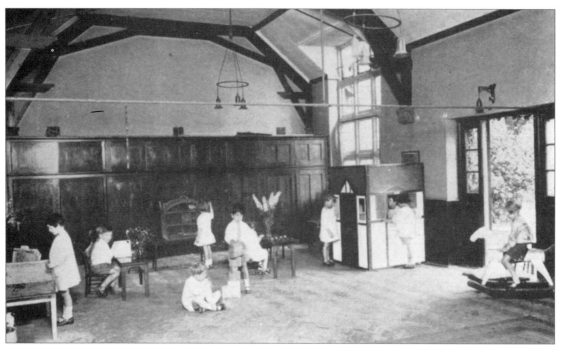

A nursery class at the Froebel Educational Institute, Colet Gardens (later Talgarth Road), *c.* 1937. The institute was established in the mid-1890s using the pioneering teaching methods of Friedrich Froebel. It consisted of a training college for teachers, a kindergarten and a school. Pupils included the artist Leon Underwood and the novelist Iris Murdoch. The usual school subjects were studied as well as music, handwork and physical training. Netball could be played on the school courts and the children were taken to Roehampton for football, cricket and nature study. After the First World War the training college moved to Roehampton, where the school joined them after the Second World War. The Royal Ballet School now occupies the buildings.

Pupils of the Invalid School at Peterborough School, 1913. This opened in 1905 in new premises erected in the boys' playground, with 55 pupils who had come from the tin building at Brook Green. The roll had increased to about 126 three years later. Pupils were brought to the school in two ambulances and a private bus, which can be seen in the photograph. A cook and two helpers provided schools meals for 'this voracious army'. The school had its own headmistress, Mrs Edith Bellamy, a trained nurse, and several voluntary helpers. The children were described in 1908 as possessing 'higher spirits and a greater sense of humour than many normal children'.

A millinery class at the Hammersmith Trade School for Girls, *c.* 1926 (right) and (below) a life class at the Hammersmith School of Building and Arts and Crafts, *c.* 1930. The Hammersmith College of Art & Building was founded in 1881 at 2 Dunsany Road, Brook Green, Hammersmith. In 1907 it moved to new and larger premises in Lime Grove. These were extended in 1928 and 1930 when the college became the Hammersmith School of Building and Arts and Crafts. Meanwhile in April 1909 the Hammersmith Trade School for Girls moved into temporary premises in the Lime Grove building. Girls were taught millinery, dressmaking and soft furnishing in addition to receiving a general education, and cookery and tailoring were later added to the curriculum. The Trade School moved into permanent premises at Lime Grove in 1915 and became the Hammersmith Technical School for Women in 1937. Another name change took place in 1951 when it became Mary Boon School and in 1959 it moved into premises vacated by West Kensington Central School, which had closed on the opening of Holland Park Comprehensive School in Kensington.

Some of the male students from the Hammersmith School of Building and Arts and Crafts who had been evacuated to Queen Square, Bath, on the outbreak of the Second World War in 1939. The city's Director of Education, A.W. Hoyle, and Councillor E. Clements welcomed the students, who can be seen here demonstrating their woodworking skills. Also in attendance were LCC Inspector R.R. Tomlinson (third from left) and the Principal of the School at Bath, N. Howdill (fourth from left). Other students from the school were evacuated to Calne, about 17 miles east of Bath. In November 1939 they presented a production of *Twelfth Night* at Calne Town Hall.

This photograph shows some of the cast appearing in Burlington School's production of Shakespeare's *A Midsummer Night's Dream* on 17, 18 and 19 December 1953. It was decided to film scenes from the play, and Mrs M.W. Stacey can be seen with the camera standing next to the Producer, Mrs P. Halliday. The part of Oberon was played by Rosalind Cohen, Titania by Stella Ananiou and Puck by Jennifer Burd. A comment in the school magazine a few months later recorded that 'Shakespeare is popular throughout the school'.

Pupils at John Aird School in Cobbold Road were all partially sighted, and Roy Pelle, with a 'friend', is pictured here in the biology lab. in June 1970. The school aimed to prepare its 120 pupils, some of whom came to Hammersmith from as far afield as St Albans and Hemel Hempstead, for living in a competitive world. Classes were small, with a maximum of 15 pupils, and when old enough the children were encouraged to travel alone on public transport and to go to the nearby shops at lunchtime to build up their confidence.

Dame Ninette de Valois, who celebrated her 100th birthday in 1998, with pupils of the Sadler's Wells Ballet School, February 1955. Dame Ninette founded a small ballet school in 1931 at the Sadler's Wells Theatre, which achieved status as a full educational establishment in 1947. In September 1947 the school, with the help of the Arts Council, moved into the old Froebel Institute in Colet Gardens, now part of Talgarth Road. The school became co-educational in 1948 and in 1956 it became the Royal Ballet School when the Queen granted it a Royal Charter. The photograph is a still from a BBC programme *Dancers of Tomorrow*, about a child whose ambition is to dance with the Sadler's Wells Ballet.

Staff and inmates at morning prayers at the Holt Yates Memorial Home for the Friendless and Fallen at Parsons Green, 1920s. Edward William Thomas, Secretary of the institution, led the prayers. The home, which occupied nos 3–7 Parsons Green, belonged to the London Female Preventative and Reformatory Institution and dated back to the 1860s. It provided accommodation for young women, who were trained for domestic service. During modernization some of the properties were demolished and the site was later occupied by the new Parsons Green Maternity Home which opened in 1937; it is now a health centre.

Members of the Women's League, one of many schemes run by the Salvation Army, at the Waterloo Street Citadel, 1912. The purpose of the tea party is not known. William Booth, founder of the Salvation Army, lived briefly in Hammersmith in 1865 in Shaftesbury Road (now Ravenscourt Road). Working as an independent revivalist he started a Christian Mission in Whitechapel in 1865, which 13 years later was to become the Salvation Army. Hammersmith was one of the earliest boroughs to have a Salvation Army Corps, based in a hall in Redmore Street until the opening of a permanent citadel in Waterloo Street (now Macbeth Street) in 1881.

Civic dignitaries, including the Mayor (Councillor H.G. Reynolds), the Town Clerk and others, gathered outside the Hammersmith and West Kensington Synagogue in Brook Green on 1 November 1953, after a special service to consecrate the standard of the Hammersmith and District branch of the Association of Jewish Ex-Servicemen and Women. The dignified and beautiful service was conducted by the Revd I.H. Levy, complemented by the fine singing of the choir and the pageantry of the standards of the other participating branches. Afterwards the Mayor spoke of the extraordinarily prompt response he had whenever he approached the branch for support in the charitable and social work of the borough.

This photograph shows a Corpus Christi procession, from Holy Trinity Church, wending its way around Brook Green, 9 June 1955. To the right members of the Guild of the Holy Sacrament can be seen with their banner and, in the background, the white dresses of those who would be taking Communion for the first time. Religious processions around the streets near the church before special services took place were once a feature of the Catholic faith. The various societies connected with the church would also participate. This practice has died out partly because of modern traffic problems and also because many feel that it is no longer necessary to display one's faith so publicly.

The last official engagement of Dr Wand, Bishop of London, before he retired was to lay the foundation stone of St Etheldreda's Church in Fulham Palace Road, 15 October 1955. Designed by Guy Biscoe, the new church was consecrated on 18 October 1958. The origins of St Etheldreda's date back to 1895 when services were held in a laundry ironing room in Gowan Avenue. The church expanded and construction of a permanent building began in Fulham Palace Road the following year. It was destroyed on 24 September 1940 after being hit by an incendiary bomb. The original plan to rebuild the bombed structure was abandoned in favour of a smaller, more intimate church.

Chapter 7
Health, Welfare, Politics &
Municipal Affairs

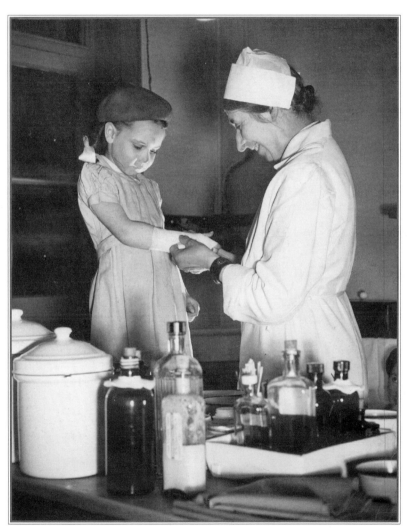

This photograph, probably taken early 1950s, is of the LCC Hammersmith School Treatment Centre at 101–3 Shepherds Bush Road, which opened *c.* 1922. The school clinic played an important part in the health and welfare of schoolchildren, but it could be a place dreaded by many, especially if they had to see the dentist. The clinics provided dental and ophthalmic services and treatment for minor ailments, foot infections and cuts and bruises. Many of these problems would be identified at a routine health inspection at school and the child could either attend the clinic or see their own doctor for treatment.

The boundaries of the constituencies which cover this borough have been revised several times since 1900. Both Hammersmith and Fulham were represented by MPs of the Conservative or similar parties, such as Unionist and Coalition Union, until the 1920s, when the growing number of working-class people living within the boroughs led to the election of Labour MPs in 1924 (Hammersmith North) and 1929 (Fulham). The only exception was the Liberal MP Timothy Davies, local shop proprietor, who was MP for Fulham 1906–10. Hammersmith's most notable MP was Sir William Bull, 1900–29, who despite his Tory credentials was a supporter of votes for women and the proposal for a Channel Tunnel. Since the Second World War the majority of MPs returned for constituencies in the borough have been Labour, although from 1979 to 1998 the Fulham area was held by the Tories. The MPs have included Dr Edith Summerskill, 1938–55 (Fulham West) and Michael Stewart, 1945-79 (Fulham East, then Fulham), who was Foreign Secretary and retired to the Lords as Lord Stewart of Fulham.

The London Government Act of 1899 abolished the vestries in Fulham and Hammersmith and replaced them with metropolitan borough councils, consisting of elected councillors who were returned every three years. The flagships of the councils were the town halls. Old Hammersmith Town Hall, in the Broadway, was opened in 1897 and superseded by the present town hall in King Street in 1939, but not pulled down until 1965. Fulham Town Hall was completed in 1890. In Fulham the Progressives, who described themselves rather unhelpfully as 'not Liberals, or Conservatives or Socialists', were the first party to take control of the Council. They were soon replaced by the Municipal Reformers who, apart from an unexpected Labour win after the First World War, retained power until 1934 when Labour won a decisive victory, one of the new councillors being Harold Laski. Labour remained the majority party until 1965, when the borough was merged with the Metropolitan Borough of Hammersmith; the first women to be elected to the Council (in 1919) were Labour, and Labour councillor Alice Gilliatt became the first woman Mayor of Fulham in 1934. In Hammersmith the Metropolitan Borough Council returned its first Labour councillors as early as 1906, and Labour took control of the Council for the first time in 1937, remaining the majority party until the metropolitan borough was amalgamated with Fulham. Since 1965, when the London Borough of Hammersmith was formed (renamed the London Borough of Hammersmith and Fulham in 1979), the Labour party has usually been the majority group on the Council, except for the 1968 and 1982 elections, which went to the Tories, and the 1978 election which gave two Liberal councillors casting votes over a hung council. In 1975 Randolph Beresford was appointed the first black Mayor of Hammersmith and Fulham.

The Fulham and Hammersmith Poor Law Union was dissolved in 1899, but the Boards of Guardians of Fulham and Hammersmith continued to exist until 1930, when their powers were taken over by the London County Council (LCC). The Guardians were responsible for administering the local hospitals that had evolved from the infirmaries of Hammersmith and Fulham workhouses. Hammersmith Hospital developed from the Hammersmith Workhouse Infirmary, built in 1905 in Du Cane Road, which was known as the Paupers' Paradise because it was considered so luxurious. After wartime use as a military hospital it was administered from 1930 onwards as a teaching hospital, specializing in orthopaedics and plastic surgery. The famous plastic surgeon Sir Archibald

MacIndoe, who treated burned airmen during the Second World War, worked at Hammersmith Hospital, and the first kidney transplant took place there in 1950. West London Hospital in Hammersmith Road, founded in 1856 and closed in 1993, was the first hospital in England to install X-ray equipment, in 1921. In 1929 Queen Charlotte's maternity hospital in central London established a branch hospital in Goldhawk Road for patients with puerperal fever. The main hospital transferred there in 1940 and after the war it was amalgamated with Chelsea Hospital for Women to form a postgraduate teaching hospital. All these hospitals became part of the National Health Service in the late 1940s. The Royal Masonic Hospital in Ravenscourt Park opened in 1933 as an independent charitable institution, initially available to freemasons and their dependants, later to other private patients. The hospital was sold in 1997 and has since reopened as another private hospital called the Stamford.

The Fulham Workhouse Infirmary was erected in Fulham Palace Road in 1883/4, and developed into a general hospital in the years before 1914. Like Hammersmith Hospital, it became a military hospital during the First World War, and many German prisoners of war were treated there. The name was changed to Fulham Hospital in 1928, and despite bomb damage on several occasions it remained open during the Second World War. Fulham Hospital was amalgamated with Charing Cross Hospital in 1959, a decision that was unpopular with Fulham people, and a large new building called Charing Cross Hospital was opened in 1973. The Western Hospital, Seagrave Road, opened in 1877 to treat smallpox and later used as a general fever hospital, became a chest hospital after the Second World War and closed in 1979.

An important feature of local government during the twentieth century has been the expansion of health and welfare services delivered by local authorities to the whole community. The role of the Medical Officer of Health was well established by the turn of the century, and attention had already been paid by the vestries and Local Boards to sewers, refuse collection and other aspects of sanitation and hygiene. The Metropolitan Boroughs of Fulham and Hammersmith both set up Public Health Committees in 1900 and Maternity and Child Welfare Committees in 1918, while the London Borough of Hammersmith formed a Social Services Committee as soon as it came into existence in 1965. The boroughs have played their part in looking after local people from cradle to grave, providing maternity services, school and children's clinics, baths and washhouses, homes for children and old people, meals on wheels and services for housebound and disabled residents. Some of these services were augmented by similar undertakings of the LCC, and by private or charitable nursing homes, orphanages and almshouses.

The dining hall at Fulham Workhouse, Fulham Palace Road, *c.* 1905. The workhouse was a place of last resort, providing food and lodging for those unable to fend for themselves, and conditions were deliberately kept harsh to discourage people from seeking entry. Fulham Workhouse was completed in 1850 and served both Fulham and Hammersmith until 1899. The murals in the dining hall, of which there were about a dozen, were painted in about 1900 by a Mr Hunter, who requested as his fee a free supply of tobacco while he worked. The site of the workhouse is now occupied by Charing Cross Hospital.

An ice-cream barrow converted into a portable soup tureen was the means by which the People's Hot Dinner Association, formed in Hammersmith in 1905, distributed hot bread and soup to all who needed it at a cost of 1*d.* For children the charge was ½*d* and steak and kidney pies could be purchased for an extra 1*d.* Food distributed by 'army reserve men out of employment' in the red and white barrows was collected from a special kitchen in Dalling Road. Elsewhere in the area, young women in need of employment prepared the vegetables for the soup.

Ward B1 at the Fulham Union Infirmary, 1913. As can be seen, the 32-bed children's ward appears to have had a high ratio of nurses to patients, and attempts have been made to brighten the bare room with flowers and a rocking-horse. Originally medical care was provided only for those in the workhouse, but gradually this provision was extended to the local community. The infirmary, which could care for up to 500 patients, was built by Messrs Gibbs & Flew, an enterprising local firm, to the designs of John Giles and Gough, architects, and formally opened on 26 June 1884.

Charing Cross Hospital in Fulham Palace Road, 24 January 1974. The Queen formally opened the hospital on 22 May 1973, about four months after it became operational and some twenty years after the initial decision to build it had been taken. The new cruciform-shaped building was erected on the site of the much-loved Fulham Hospital, which had started life as the Fulham Workhouse and Infirmary, and its construction involved the demolition of three neighbouring streets. Work on the new hospital, designed by Ralph Tubbs, began in 1968 and the topping-out ceremony took place on 15 April 1970. It was the first teaching hospital to be built and opened since the Second World War.

Nurses in the grounds of Western Hospital, Seagrave Road, Fulham, *c.* 1905. The hospital, which opened on 10 March 1877 as the Fulham Smallpox Hospital, took patients from all over London. Initially the nurses were male, but this changed a few months later when women patients started to be accepted. There were 10 pavilions, 8 housing patients and 2 used as dormitories for nurses and attendants. It was extended several times, against much opposition, and accepted its last smallpox patients in 1885. Renamed Western Hospital in 1883, it continued to be used as an isolation hospital for many years and was also a centre for the mass X-ray service. The hospital closed in 1979 and the 8 acre site was built over.

A bemused young patient at the Royal Masonic Hospital, Hammersmith, meeting HRH the Crown Prince of Saudi Arabia, summer 1935. The freemasons' hospital was opened on 12 July 1933 by King George V, accompanied by Queen Mary, and replaced an earlier hospital at 237 Fulham Road. The architects for the new hospital were Messrs Sir John Burnet, RA, Tait and Lorne, and the contractors were Messrs John Mowlem & Co. Ltd. The hospital closed in the mid-1990s but has reopened since as The Stamford.

Thousands lined the streets of Fulham to see their Carnival Queen drive in procession to Fulham Palace for the fifth annual garden party organized by the Friends of Fulham Hospital, 1 July 1961. The event raised about £500 for comforts for patients at the hospital. The Fulham Band, which was supposed to lead the procession, was unable to muster enough players and was replaced by the DER television rental company's open-topped bus, which was equipped with a loudspeaker to play music. There was a motorcade of over 20 vehicles including the float pictured here, entered by the Council's Public Health Department and winners of the second prize in the group for local traders and Council departments.

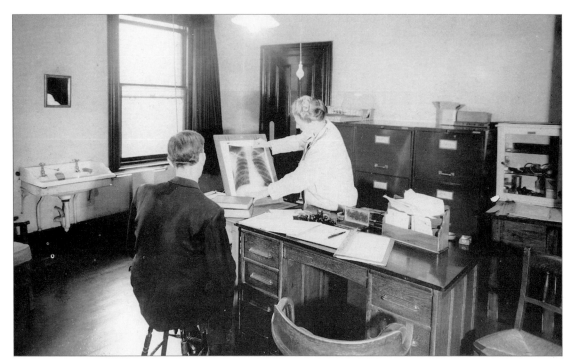

One method of detecting tuberculosis was the X-ray, as can be seen here at the Fulham Chest Clinic, formerly the Fulham Dispensary for Consumption, at 114 New Kings Road, *c.* 1950. Tuberculosis, an insidious disease made worse by poor living and working conditions, could often be cured if caught in time. The first dispensary opened at 632 Fulham Road on 1 November 1911 and three years later moved to New Kings Road. In 1950 there were 42 deaths from tuberculosis in Fulham and 228 cases were notified. An X-ray service was later opened at Western Hospital in Seagrave Road, enabling 9–10,000 investigations to be carried out each year.

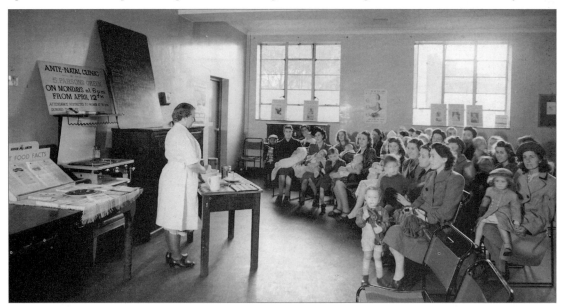

A cookery lesson at the Parsons Green Maternity Home and Clinic, Fulham, *c.* 1950. Special classes for mothers giving advice on feeding and all aspects of childcare were among the services provided there. The maternity home opened in October 1937, replacing earlier premises located in a converted house in Fulham Road. There was provision for 25 beds in small wards containing between 2 and 6 beds. In the clinic, dental facilities were available as well as artificial sunlight treatment and a dispensary for the distribution of babies' foods.

Disabled soldiers at the Special Military Surgical Hospital, Du Cane Road, Hammersmith, *c.* 1918. Formerly the Hammersmith Workhouse Infirmary, this special hospital was set up to treat disabled soldiers and to teach them a trade. Men were taught leatherwork, carpentry, printing, tailoring and even welding. In this photograph they are shown rolling cigarettes. The hospital closed at the end of March 1922 as the Ministry of Pensions refused to pay the rent increase from £8,000 to £14,000 proposed by Hammersmith Borough Council. At the time of closure there were about 700 inpatients and a large number of outpatients.

Mattresses being loaded into a van after disinfection at the Hammersmith Medicinal Baths in Scotts Road, *c.* 1957. Hammersmith Borough Council's Public Health Department had many duties, including supervision of food supplies, monitoring of industrial emissions, inspection of factories and shops, rodent control, provision of a mortuary, provision of personal health services and prevention of the spread of diseases. Cleansing stations were provided where persons suffering from scabies and other infectious diseases could be treated and clothing could be disinfected.

The Fulham Wasteland and Lygon Almshouses, Fulham Palace Road, 1947. Almshouses were an early form of sheltered housing, providing homes, perhaps with a warden, and often fuel and a small income too for the occupants. The first of the Wasteland Almshouses was built in 1833 on the corner of Dawes and Estcourt Roads at a cost of £896 and extended four years later. In 1884 land known as Lygon's Acre was acquired and the almshouses seen to the left and back of this picture were built in 1886. They were extended to the designs of Ernest Avern in 1906, after a vigorous fundraising campaign. The almshouses were rebuilt in 1980.

The actor John Le Mesurier was the star attraction at a special late-night evening opening of shops in King Street, Hammersmith, for shoppers with disabilities, 10 June 1971. Taken at Marks & Spencer, the photograph shows from left to right: Miss Sparks 1971, the Mayor (Councillor Tom Morris), Mrs Annette Goodwin and John Le Mesurier. Woolworth's, Boots, Marks & Spencer and the Co-op opened their doors to 200 people using wheelchairs, and their friends. The event was organized by the Rotary Club, and volunteers from local schools, Council staff, police cadets and staff from George Wimpey gave their time from 6 p.m. to 8 p.m. to help.

This photograph was taken in 1949 to demonstrate the work of Hammersmith Borough Council's Finance Department. It shows Mr K. Perry, of the Rates Department, with a local resident paying her rates and rent. The large volume on the desk is a ratebook, recording all rateable property in the borough, the names of ratepayers, details of rateable values, types of property and the sums of money due. The rates in 1949 were 16s 10d (about 84p) in the pound, based largely on property size and facilities. For example, a property with central heating or a garage would be rated more highly than an adjacent one without. Today's equivalent to the rates is the Council Tax.

Twynholm Orphanage, 710 Fulham Road, c. 1915. The orphanage, founded by Sydney Black in rooms at the top of Twynholm House, Fulham Cross, opened June 1893. With more space needed, a move to 156 Lillie Road followed, and after the death of Black in 1903 there was another move to 710 Fulham Road. Subsequently additional premises at 712 Fulham Road were acquired. The orphanage closed in January 1939 when it merged with Spurgeon's Orphanage and the children moved to Stockwell. Initially only boys were admitted and 172 of them were cared for at the home before its closure. Later, between 1918 and 1939, a total of 52 girls were admitted.

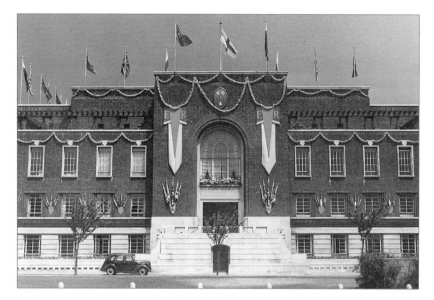

The river frontage of Hammersmith Town Hall displaying a fine array of flags in celebration of the coronation of Queen Elizabeth II, 2 June 1953. Hammersmith Borough Council had voted to spend £2,000 on decorating Council buildings and £2,000 on decorating the main roads in the borough. The town hall, which replaced an earlier building in Brook Green Road, had been completed just after the outbreak of the Second World War to the designs of E. Berry Webber. The building was described as 'resplendent with golden banners and flags' and King Street as 'the best decorated part of the West London route' taken by the new Queen and the Duke of Edinburgh on their coronation drive.

Councillor Randolph Beresford, the first black Mayor of Hammersmith & Fulham, seen here receiving his chain of office from former Mayor George Simpson on 21 May 1975. Mr Beresford, a skilled carpenter by trade, came to Shepherds Bush from Guyana in 1953. An active trade unionist in the Amalgamated Society of Woodworkers, he served the borough as a councillor from 1964 to 1982. At the time he was elected Mayor he was Trade Steward and Convenor for the Greater London Council Western District and Joint Secretary to the District Joint Consultative Committee. He was awarded the British Empire Medal (BEM) in 1979 for outstanding service and appointed a Member of the British Empire (MBE) in 1987.

Fulham's first female Mayor, Alice Gilliatt, November 1934. Miss Gilliatt, after whom a small housing estate in Star Road is named, was a pharmacist at the Western Hospital. Prior to joining the Labour Party she was a member of the Suffragette Movement. As a member of Fulham Borough Council 1919–22 and 1934–53 she was particularly interested in the Council's health services. She was known as the 'cycling mayor', cycling everywhere to keep her engagements, and was ahead of her time in stating that during her year as Mayor 'no robes whatever shall be worn . . . but I shall, of course, wear the chain of office'.

William Bull (1863–1931) was MP for
Hammersmith 1900–18 and Hammersmith
South 1918–29. He started his career as a
solicitor in the family firm of Bull & Bull. He
served on the LCC for nine years from 1892
and began his parliamentary career in 1900.
Among his various interests was the Channel
Tunnel, which he was convinced would be
built eventually, and he served as Chairman of
the House of Commons Channel Tunnel
Committee. He was knighted in 1905, became
a Privy Councillor in 1918 and a Baronet in
1922. He is pictured here, seated centre, with
party workers at their Hammersmith
Committee Rooms, 2 The Broadway, preparing
for the 1922 General Election.

Michael Stewart (1906–83) was MP for East Fulham
1945–55 and for Fulham 1955–79, and on retiring from
the Commons took his seat in the House of Lords as Lord
Stewart of Fulham. Between 1930 and 1942 he taught at
Merchant Taylors' School and at the Coopers' Company's
School. During the Second World War he joined the Army
Intelligence Corps and was transferred in 1943 to the
Educational Corps. Meanwhile he had unsuccessfully
contested West Lewisham as a Labour candidate in 1930
and 1935. During his years as an MP he held office as
Secretary of State for three different departments –
Education, the Foreign Office and Economic Affairs. He was
given the Freedom of the Borough in 1967.

'Petticoat politics: amusing scenes at Hammersmith' is the
caption to this illustration in the *Daily Graphic*, 25 May 1906.
The subject of the photograph is Miss Billington speaking at a
demonstration in favour of Mrs Dora Montefiore of Clare
Lodge, Upper Mall, Hammersmith, who was refusing to pay
income tax as a 'protest against the exclusion of women from
the Parliamentary franchise'. She believed that 'taxation
without representation is tyranny'. Another demonstration
was held the following month attended by 60 women of the
working class who had come from Canning Town to support
the rebel. Women aged 30 and over received the vote in
1918, and the franchise was further extended to women over
21 in 1928.

Sewer works in Everington Street, Fulham, 14 October 1957. They took seven months to complete and started at the Lillie Road junction. As the trench was so deep a heavy motorized crane had to be used 'for pitching and drawing the sheeting and raising excavated material', resulting in major damage to the clinker asphalt surface of the road. A new manhole was built at the head of the sewer, and badly corroded and dangerous sets of step irons were replaced in five locations before the road was resurfaced.

Fulham Power Station in Townmead Road, probably late 1940s. The first of Fulham Borough Council's power stations opened in 1901. During its first year of operation 407,256 units of electricity were sold and in the year ended 31 March 1936, before the new station opened, demand had risen so much that 32,614,969 units were sold. The new power station, which was extended several times, opened 26 September 1936 on a site adjacent to the old one, which was subsequently used as a coal store. The power station was nationalized in 1948 and closed 30 years later. Demolition began in 1983 and the Harbour Club now occupies the site.

Above, a mobile refuse container, located in Racton Road, Fulham, for use by the traders in the North End Road Market, 1950s. Below, a Hammersmith Borough Council dustcart and its jolly crew in an unidentified location, 1952. The collection of refuse is an important function carried out by the borough councils. In Hammersmith and Fulham not only is refuse collected from shops, offices and nearly 75,000 households, but also from the street markets. Over the years a variety of vehicles have been developed for this purpose, including dustless loading models, enabling the dustmen to avoid physical contact with the refuse. These are now capable of lifting large bins from blocks of flats and offices, emptying their contents into the vehicle and crushing the contents. The latest vehicle is appropriately known as a 'Vulture'. One very useful service, in operation for about the last 20 years, is the weekend skip service, which enables residents to get rid of larger items of household rubbish that cannot be collected as part of the routine refuse collection.

A post-war library under construction, *c.* 1964. Barons Court Library started life in temporary shop premises at 70 North End Road in June 1940, and moved to a prefabricated building at North End Crescent in October 1949. Fulham Borough Council's Architect, E.G. Sames, designed this octagonal building to replace it. Construction took 10 months and the Mayor, Councillor J.J. Ireland, opened the new library, which cost £60,000 and contained 10,500 books, on 10 July 1965. The Council had embarked on a programme of modernization of all its libraries in 1960 and by the end of 1965 had completed work on the Fulham Central Library and four branch libraries.

The reference library at Hammersmith Central Library, 1950s. The library, the gift of Andrew Carnegie, was designed by Henry T. Hare and officially opened on 24 July 1905. Two other libraries, at Ravenscourt Park and Shepherds Bush, were already in use in the borough in addition to a temporary reading room opposite the new building. The reference library, on the first floor, provided seating for 72 persons. The stained-glass window, seen in this photograph, contains the Borough's arms and those of Sir Nicholas Crisp, and at the opposite end of the room another window contains a full-length portrait of Dean Colet.

An enthusiastic audience listening to a pipe band at the Bishops Park Open Air Theatre, 1974. The theatre, designed by E.A.H. Macdonald for Fulham Borough Council, was opened on 2 July 1960. It provided a wide range of entertainment for local residents, including jazz and orchestral concerts, opera, plays, old time music hall, talent shows and performances from local schools of dancing. The theatre was set in beautiful surroundings but events could be marred by intrusive noise from aircraft and from pleasure boats on the Thames. In December 1991 the theatre was gutted by fire and it was demolished in March 1994.

During Road Safety Week, August 1952, cycling proficiency tests and road safety games took place in Bishops Park (seen here), South Park and Lillie Road Recreation Ground. Hundreds of children attended with their parents, watched a special programme of safety plays performed by the Field Puppets, and were tested on careful riding skills and on their knowledge of the Highway Code. One common fault of the young cyclists was that they tended to ride using only one hand on the handlebars and with their fingers too far from the brakes. Special prizes and pennants were awarded to the successful entrants.

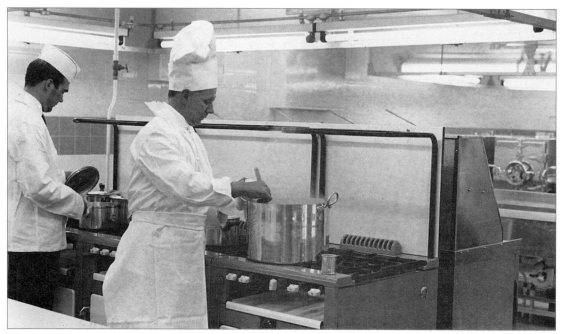

The opening of the Milson Road Central Service Kitchen, Hammersmith, took place on 6 September 1965. It was built at a cost of £70,000 and was the first municipal kitchen in the country to be devoted solely to the provision of meals for the meals on wheels service. It was anticipated that 1,200 meals a day would be provided. The building, which was 60 years old and had originally been a dairy, had most recently been used as a transport depot and stores department. Chef David Buchanan is seen here preparing some of the food needed that day.

This photograph was taken in September 1974 in London's first self-contained purpose-built Register Office in Hammersmith, located in Nigel Playfair Avenue, after the marriage of Jasmine Johnson and Wilfred Barry. The bride came from Shepherds Bush and her groom from the Virgin Islands where the couple planned to make their home. The new office cost about £100,000 to build and was designed by the Borough Architect, R.A. Mitchelmore. The building was planned to give a 'sense of importance of occasion rather than the feeling of being part of a production line'.

Chapter 8
Wartime

Capt. Richard Wakeford. Son of Dr V.D.C. Wakeford of 728 Fulham Road, he won his VC while in action at Cassino in Italy on 13/14 May 1944, sustaining injuries to his face and all four limbs. He was decorated 'on the field' by King George VI, and presented with a medal in a ceremony at Buckingham Palace in December of that year while home on a month's leave. His mother was asked by a reporter from the *Fulham Chronicle* how she liked having her gallant 23-year-old son home on leave for the first time in two years. She replied, 'I like it very much, but with him sitting there I daren't say any more.'

The Boer War (1899–1902) was in progress when the century opened, but this remote war in South Africa did not directly affect Hammersmith and Fulham. Only 12 years later local people had to face the realities of world conflict. War with Germany was declared on 4 August 1914, and soon thousands of Belgian refugees arrived and were accommodated at Earls Court, the White City and in houses around the boroughs. Emergency recruiting centres opened in venues such as Fulham County School, although conscription did not start until early 1916. The Territorials were mobilized and soldiers camped in Bishops Park and other open spaces.

Local industries played their part in the First World War. The Alliance Aeroplane Co. made aeroplanes in the former Waring and Gillow factory in Cambridge Grove, Blakes ammunition factory was in Wood Lane and munitions were made at Wormwood Scrubs. White City was particularly busy, accommodating training and recruitment activities as well as up to 8,000 people manufacturing tents, gas masks and other military equipment. Fulham Pottery made rum jars for the armed forces, fragments of which, lost during the Gallipoli landings, have been found in Turkey. J. Lyons and Co. sent vans from Cadby Hall in Hammersmith to help ferry wounded soldiers from Waterloo station to London hospitals after the first Battle of Ypres. During the First World War many women were employed in place of men who had gone to serve, a development which led directly to their admittance at last to the franchise in 1918.

Both Fulham and Hammersmith Workhouse Infirmaries became military hospitals, the latter specializing in orthopaedics, while Fulham Palace took in convalescent officers. Municipal kitchens were set up at Victoria Hall, Becklow Road, and at Lime Grove Baths, and land such as the meadow at Fulham Palace and part of South Park was turned into allotments to increase food production. Food rationing was not introduced until 1918, and the blackout was merely a dimming of lights rather than total darkness. No Zeppelin raids took place in the boroughs, and altogether the inconvenience to civilians caused by the war seems to have been minor compared with the Second World War. But the lists of casualties in the local newspapers are a reminder of the high price which many families had to pay in the killing fields of Ypres, the Somme and Passchendaele.

By 1938 it was clear that another war with Germany was likely. Local authorities were responsible for air raid precautions (ARP) and made preparations accordingly, convening Emergency Committees and establishing control centres in Fulham and Hammersmith Town Halls. ARP wardens' posts and first-aid stations were set up, heavy rescue teams formed and plans made for fire-fighting, and in early 1939 Anderson air raid shelters, which could be dug into back gardens, became available. Sand was extracted from local parks for sandbags and gas masks distributed. War became inevitable when Hitler invaded Poland on Friday 1 September 1939, the same day that the LCC ordered the immediate evacuation of local schools and the blackout was first enforced. The actual declaration of war on Sunday 3 September at 11.15 a.m. must have been almost a relief.

For some months, during the period of the 'phoney war', nothing much happened. Schools in the borough were evacuated to such places as Guildford, Haslemere, High Wycombe, Midhurst (Lady Margaret School) and Easthampstead (St Paul's Boys' School). By the following summer local schools were reopening and children drifting back from the country, although throughout the war the population of both boroughs remained much lower than usual. Food rationing started in January 1940.

On 7 September 1940 the period of sustained air raids known as the Blitz began and continued until the following May. Hammersmith and Fulham did not suffer as badly as some other Metropolitan Boroughs, but nevertheless took many devastating hits. In Fulham, 10 ARP workers were killed at St Dionis Road in Fulham's first air raids on 9 September 1940, 38 people died in an air raid shelter in Bucklers Alley on 13 September, and 20 at Greyhound Road on the night of 15/16 November. In Hammersmith, 9 people were killed at Starfield Road on 18 September 1940, 21 at Askew Road a week later, 20 when the Telegraph pub in Richmond Gardens was destroyed on 26 October and on 3 December a bomb fell on a public air raid shelter at the convent of the Misericorde Sisters and killed 42 people. These were just some of the worst incidents. The air raids caused extensive damage to houses and many people were made homeless and had to be given emergency accommodation while the local authorities struggled to keep up with repairs. Fulham Power Station and Gas Works were particularly important targets for the bombers, and anti-aircraft guns, searchlights and barrage balloons were stationed at Hurlingham Club.

As in the First World War, many local industries concentrated on manufacturing war equipment, such as the small reconnaissance airships (blimps) which were made at Wormwood Scrubs. Allotments again became popular, the No. 1 polo ground at Hurlingham Club being dug up for that purpose. Everyone carried National Registration cards, petrol and clothes rationing were introduced in 1939 and 1941, and as the food ration dwindled British restaurants and Londoners' Meals Service centres providing cheap meals were set up in premises such as the former Timothy Davies shop at 2–6 Fulham Broadway. To prevent inflation, people were encouraged to save through a series of savings weeks, including Wings for Victory and Salute the Soldier.

By 1944 the invasion of Europe was being planned at St Paul's School in Hammersmith, which had become the headquarters of the 21st Army Group. Meanwhile some bad conventional air raids in February 1944 were followed by attacks by the new flying bombs (V1s) in June. The V1s killed 15 people at Lintaine Grove on 18 June 1944, another 15 in Avalon Road on 1 July and 12 at Cromwell Mansions on 2 July. None of the final wave of airborne missiles, the V2 rockets, fell in Fulham, but in Hammersmith the Cleverly estate was hit. The end of the war was in sight, as the Allies were advancing on all fronts in the months after D-Day (6 June 1944). VE (Victory in Europe) Day was finally celebrated on 8 May 1945, and many local street parties were held in the following weeks.

This photograph of the First World War Recruiting Office at Fulham Town Hall is thought to date from about May 1916, as before that date only unmarried men between the ages of 18 and 40 could be conscripted. Posters on the wall give details of separation allowances for the wives and children of soldiers. Initially Fulham County School was requisitioned in August 1914 as an emergency recruiting station, and the headmistress had great difficulty persuading the occupiers to move out to Fulham Town Hall before the start of term at the end of September. The town hall was used as a recruiting office for the rest of the war, and many offices there and in the neighbourhood were occupied by the Army.

Several rolls of honour were published in the 1915 issues of the *Peterborough School Magazine*. This page from the April issue portrays eighteen of the school's former pupils who were serving in the forces or contributing in some way to the war effort. The list of names accompanying the photographs includes what appear to be two brothers from one family and a brother and sister from another – Arthur and Alan Birch who were serving in the Grenadier Guards and Royal Engineers respectively, and Margaret and J.F. Rumble who were serving as a nurse and in the 2nd Middlesex Regiment respectively.

About 3,000 Belgian refugees found shelter and accommodation in the Empress Hall at Earls Court during the First World War, while others were billeted with local residents. Some of the children were educated at Earls Court, as seen in this photograph, or at Fulham County School, and other places were found for about 300 children at St Thomas of Canterbury RC School. Plaques commemorating their stay in Fulham and their link with St Thomas' School and Church were erected at Fulham Town Hall and at the church.

The purpose of this procession by young female Belgian refugees is not known, but as the banners are of a religious nature they may be celebrating a saint's day, perhaps that of St Thomas of Canterbury on 3 July. The photograph was taken in Fulham Road near the junction with Parsons Green Lane, July 1918. Unfortunately the event was not covered in the local newspapers.

The top photograph is thought to have been taken at the First World War municipal kitchen at Victoria Hall, Becklow Road, and the centre one shows the delivery vans associated with the scheme. Hammersmith was the first London borough to set up a municipal kitchen with distribution centres during the war, providing cooked food at reasonable prices without incurring financial loss. This scheme was felt to be particularly important for children whose mothers were engaged in war work away from home and could not cook for them. The first distribution centre and kitchen opened at the Victoria Hall in May 1917, on an experimental basis, when 800 meals were served on the first day and 2,000 the next. Menus changed weekly and included kidney soup, mutton pies, jam roll, etc. Purchasers brought their own containers for the generous portions served. Two Ford motor delivery vans with soft-tops costing £134 each were purchased to ferry the food between the kitchens and distribution centres. Eventually several kitchens and centres were in action and remained open until 29 March 1919, shortly after the war ended.

Employees of Fulham Borough Council's Electricity Department in the yard at Argon Mews, probably shortly after the outbreak of war in 1939. Some of the men in this photograph may have enrolled to serve in a Corps of Local Defence Volunteers set up to protect the Council's power station against damage by German parachute troops. Argon Mews was hit by an incendiary bomb in the early hours of 26 September 1940, at the height of the Blitz. This was only one of 64 incidents recorded that day when bombs rained over the borough. Plans were approved for a decontamination centre in the mews in October 1939 and later, in June 1942, for an air raid shelter and a women's rest room.

The artist of this amusing watercolour, John Thorn, served during the Second World War as an air raid warden. During his limited spare time he produced a number of drawings of events and people's reactions to them. This one, entitled *Troglodites*, shows the residents of Sussex Place, near Hammersmith Bridge, entering an air raid shelter during the Blitz, September 1940. They can be seen with their gas masks, bedding, food and drink, toys and even a goldfish in a bowl. The artist noted on the back of the picture that nearly all those depicted were real people and that he executed it while on duty as a shelter marshal.

Faulty air raid shelters at the Guinness Trust Buildings, *c.* 1942. Following the deaths of two people in a shelter which collapsed in Macfarlane Road, a number of other shelters in Hammersmith were found to be defective. The builder and his clerk of works were found not guilty of manslaughter but were imprisoned for nine months on charges of conspiracy to defraud the Council of £25,119 and of false pretences. They had built 120 shelters with faulty roofs in Hammersmith between May 1940 and March 1941. Ninety-nine shelters had their roofs removed, and it was found that the thickness of the concrete was only 3 in instead of 5 in.

The devastation caused after a direct hit by a flying bomb (V1) on flats in Peabody Estate, Fulham Palace Road, in the early hours of 22 August 1944. Many were killed and injured but luckily the majority of residents were in the air raid shelters in the courtyard. Stella Fowler, a library assistant, commented: 'We heard the bomb coming and covered our heads with the bedclothes. Then there was a terrific crash and we were smothered in debris. The rescue workers got us out and carried my mother down the tottering staircase.' Another resident's husband had insisted that they went to the shelter. 'I shudder to think what might have happened to us had we not been in the shelter.'

Members of the YWCA Youth Club based at Hampshire House in Hampshire Hog Lane responded rapidly after their premises were bombed on 15 June 1943. Luckily the high-explosive bomb only partially exploded and the four occupants of the house escaped with minor injuries and shock. Club meetings resumed within two weeks and restoration work on the Georgian property was carried out in 1946. There had been plans to demolish the house before the war to make way for the Cromwell Road extension. The war brought a temporary reprieve but it was eventually demolished and the Great West Road built across its site.

Fulham's Warship Week in 1942 aimed to raise
£700,000 (or £10 per head of population) to buy
HMS *Relentless*. The event raised £932,401 through
band concerts, an international wrestling match, a
treasure hunt, civil defence exercises and a naval
exhibition. A replica of the forecastle of the ship was
built in Fulham Broadway from salvaged timber, and the
former store of Messrs Timothy Davies was transformed
into an exhibition centre. On display were exhibits of
torpedoes, models of old ships, a replica of a modern
warship and a power-driven gun turret which visitors
could work themselves. The star attraction was a
specially constructed static water tank in which
practical demonstrations of submarine escapes took
place four times daily.

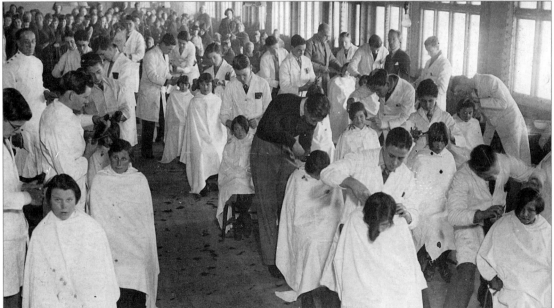

This photograph, published in the *Weston Mercury and Somersetshire Herald* in January 1940, shows trainee
hairdressers from the Regent Street Polytechnic, who had been evacuated to Weston-super-Mare, cutting the
hair of girls from Brackenbury Road School. Children from the school had been evacuated to Somerset on the
outbreak of war. Most went to Frome, some to Weston-super-Mare, but many returned to London after a few
months when the danger seemed to have lessened.

The children of Addison Gardens School, Hammersmith, were evacuated in September 1939 to various locations in Buckinghamshire, including Maids Moreton, Akeley, Chackmore, Thornborough, Turweston, Padbury and High Wycombe. Many of the children had never been in the countryside before and were astounded at 'feeling so much space around them and so much grass'. At Maids Moreton lessons were held in the village hall and the female pupils, pictured here in January 1940, can be seen listening to a BBC radio broadcast for schools. Later that month many of the pupils appeared in a nativity play at the hall.

Peace Day at Hurlingham Club, September 1919. Although Peace Day at the end of the First World War was held on 19 July 1919, Fulham councillors decided to have two special days of celebrations on 16 and 17 September for children, either at their schools or, for older pupils, on the No. 2 polo ground at the Hurlingham Club. The club grounds were turned each day into a playground with swings, roundabouts and all kinds of novel amusements. There were organized sports with prizes, and pupils were given three 1d vouchers to exchange for fruit, ice cream or sweets. The cost of entertaining some 28,000 children came to £1,000.

Chapter 9
Special Events

Raising money to endow beds at West London Hospital by the novel means of the 'million penny fund', 1925. The Mayor of Hammersmith, Alderman C. Pascall, obtained 500 new pennies from the Mint and got his grandchildren, pictured here, to lay the first of many coins on the hospital steps on Boxing Day 1925. Troughs were set up by the roadside to take the donations of passers-by. Up to 6 January 1926 a total of 180,097 pennies in the form of coins, stamps and cheques had been collected.

Photographs of public events in Hammersmith and Fulham over the last 100 years bear witness to the changing nature of society. Before the advent of television, large crowds were prepared to turn out to see a minor screen star arriving to open an exhibition, or the Mayor inaugurating a new park or civic building. Poverty impelled the elderly or children to take advantage en masse of free dinners and tea parties. Lack of traffic made street processions possible, and people spent months preparing elaborate pageants and other open-air events.

Royal visits were great occasions in those days, with crowds lining the streets. Notable royal visitors to the borough include the Prince and Princess of Wales in 1902, on the occasion of the King's Dinner to the Poor, at which 14,000 people were fed roast beef and plum pudding on 2½ miles of tables in Bishops Park; King George V and Queen Mary, who drove through Fulham and Hammersmith on 8 June 1935 to mark their Silver Jubilee; and King George VI and Queen Elizabeth, who visited the borough in February 1944 to view bomb damage. The recent change in public perception of the royal family and their role in modern Britain may mean that the street parties and other local celebrations of the Queen's Silver Jubilee in 1977 were the last of their kind. Perhaps the next coronation will still cause excitement, but it is unlikely to be marked by events like the King's Dinner to the Poor, which was in honour of King Edward VII's coronation, or the tea parties for pensioners held in Fulham Town Hall in 1937 for King George VI's coronation. These events called for a great deal of organization and preparation, and even more was demanded by the English Church Pageant, which took place at Fulham Palace in 1909 with a cast of 4,000 people from all over London, with the aim of raising money for the Church. A year later the Army Pageant was held at Fulham Palace, in aid of a servicemen's charity. Thousands of troops, a choir of 300 and a band of 200 were involved in a spectacle which included a re-enactment of the Battle of Naseby.

Local authorities, their powers and budgets not yet shorn by central government, exercised a more significant and paternalistic influence over the daily lives of local people than they do now. The Metropolitan Borough Councils of Hammersmith and Fulham were prepared to mount large exhibitions on topics of civic importance, such as the need to reduce fuel consumption in 1947 and the new Clean Air Act in 1956. The public were not always as interested as might have been wished. The Council also encouraged and participated in special initiatives and street collections for charity, such as the million penny fund in 1925, which raised money to endow beds at West London Hospital. In the end only half a million pennies were collected (about £2,000).

People's desire to see celebrities in the flesh is as old as human nature, the only thing that has changed being the type of celebrity. Pop stars and footballers are now idolized more than aviators and heroic soldiers. Yuri Gagarin, the Russian cosmonaut who was the first man in space, made a world tour after his flight and was greeted everywhere as a hero and pop star rolled into one. He came briefly to Hammersmith to visit Earls Court Exhibition Centre on 11 July 1961. The aviator Claude Grahame-White, who built a biplane at Wormwood Scrubs in 1910, was another celebrity of his day, as were so many early aviators. It was common too for stars of stage and screen to be invited to lay foundation stones or open buildings, particularly cinemas. The American film star

Tallulah Bankhead, for example, laid the foundation stone of the Commodore Cinema in King Street in 1929 (now demolished). During both wars, and in particular the Second World War, famous servicemen of high rank or ordinary soldiers who had received the Victoria Cross sometimes visited in order to raise morale and encourage people in the war effort. One very eminent soldier, Field Marshal Montgomery, had worked at St Paul's School (his old school) planning the D-Day invasion of Europe, and he returned to Hammersmith on 5 March 1949 to receive the Freedom of Hammersmith.

The Oxford and Cambridge University boat race used to be extremely popular with people from all walks of life, and old photographs from the early 1900s testify to the crowds around Hammersmith Bridge (and dangerously perched all over it). Interest in the boat race has waned, but the passion which people feel for their football team remains unchanged and indeed has grown in the last decade, thanks to intensive marketing and promotion of the game. Two of the most momentous events of the twentieth century, the signing of the Armistice in 1918 and the announcement of VE Day in 1945, brought people out into the streets in a way which rarely happens nowadays. Perhaps the only comparable gatherings are the celebrations after a local team wins the FA Cup.

The plane shown here being constructed in the hangar at Wormwood Scrubs belonged to the aviator Claude Grahame-White, competing in the London–Manchester Aeroplane Race in April 1910 for a prize of £10,000. On arrival at Wormwood Scrubs with his dismantled Henry Farman biplane on a lorry, 'immense crowds surveyed with awe its slender frame of varnished wood, its frail linen covered wings, its yards of piano wire, brass petrol tanks and gleaming Gnome engine'. On his first attempt on 23 April he got as far as Lichfield, and four days later to Poleworth, but the race was won by Louis Paulham who had flown from Hendon. Wormwood Scrubs continued as an aviation ground for several years after the race.

Crowds starting to assemble in Hammersmith Broadway at 11.50 a.m. on 11 November 1918 as news spread that the First World War had ended. The Armistice signed that morning at 5 a.m. (French time) came into force six hours later at 11 a.m. The Mayor, Alderman Henry J. Foreman, read a statement from the steps of Hammersmith Town Hall to councillors and a large number of the borough's residents. Little work was done that day as people rushed into the streets from their homes, offices and shops, and buses and taxis were filled with people cheering and waving flags. There was a profound sense of relief that the long and dreadful war had at last ended.

Collectors for Alexandra Rose Day outside Barons Court station, 25 June 1919. The day, named after Queen Alexandra, consort of King Edward VII, was devoted to the raising of funds in aid of hospitals. In 1919 140 sellers, all female, collected the sum of £435 in Fulham, backed up by another 11 workers in the depots. Afterwards the Mayoress, Lady Norris, entertained them to tea at Fulham Town Hall. The sellers in the photograph are, from left to right: Mrs Gatton, Mrs Falcon, Miss W. Broom and Mrs Thornborough.

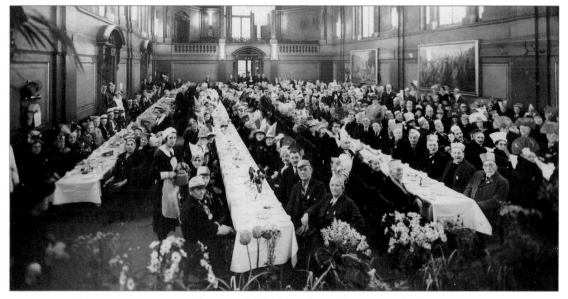

Two parties for 600 pensioners each, one of which is shown here, were held at Fulham Town Hall to celebrate the coronation of King George VI and Queen Elizabeth in May 1937. A bus strike on the day of one of the parties meant that many had a long walk to Walham Green, and the *Fulham Chronicle* reported that 'it was pathetic to see some of them hobbling along with the aid of sticks'. The luckier inmates of the Fulham Institution were conveyed in LCC motor ambulances. The tea, which was estimated to cost 1*s* 3*d* (about 6p) per person, included sandwiches that 'were so dainty that those who had long ago lost their molars had not the slightest fear of digestive disturbance'.

Erecting a triumphal arch, one of two through which the Prince and Princess of Wales passed en route to the King's Dinner to the Poor, held in Bishops Park on 5 July 1902 to celebrate the coronation of Edward VII. The costs of the arches was shared between Fulham Borough Council and the nearby Grand Theatre. Some 14,000 guests, who brought their own cutlery, dined together en masse assisted by 2,000 servers; the meal included roast beef and plum pudding. Arrangements were made for 400 meals to be delivered to those too infirm to attend, and the helpers received gifts of the King's special souvenir card and a box of chocolate.

The opening of the first Hammersmith Town Hall in Brook Green Road was performed by the Duke and Duchess of Fife on 22 July 1897. The building, designed by J.H. Richardson and constructed by Messrs Wimpey, was not quite finished. On their arrival in an open carriage, the Duke and Duchess were greeted by enthusiastic crowds of people lining the road and by the drum and fife band of the 2nd South Middlesex Volunteers, who also provided the guard of honour. They were received at the entrance to the octagonal hall by the chairman of the vestry and others, and conducted to the reception room before proceeding to the large hall for the ceremony.

Craftsman R.Osborne and L/Cpl Goodfield unloading petrol at a garage near 'The Seven Stars' in Goldhawk Road during the 1953 petrol strike. The short unofficial strike between 20 and 27 October 1953 by over 2,500 petrol tanker crews created many problems not only for motorists but for other services such as public transport, undertakers, doctors, refuse collectors and bakers. The Army and RAF were called in to drive the tankers after the strikers rejected an appeal from their union to return to work. Two days later the strikers agreed to return to work if the servicemen withdrew. Petrol deliveries resumed on 27 October.

Major Yuri Gagarin, the Russian cosmonaut and first man in space, made an official visit to Great Britain in July 1961. He was met at London Airport, now Heathrow, on 11 July and driven to the Russian Embassy in an open car with the appropriate numberplate of YG 1. Enthusiastic crowds greeted his arrival. In the afternoon he visited the Russian Exhibition at Earls Court where a model of a spaceship was on view. While in Great Britain he had lunch with the Queen, met the Prime Minister Harold Macmillan, visited a foundry in Manchester and did some London sightseeing. This photograph shows him in his car outside 227 Hammersmith Road on the day of his arrival.

A crowd awaiting the arrival of Jane Carr, the screen and stage star of the day, at Fulham's Fuel Economy
Campaign Exhibition at Fulham Central Library. The Fuel Economy Campaign, 16–30 August 1947, was part
of a national campaign to reduce fuel consumption by 25 per cent. The exhibition was entered via a life-size
model of a pit gallery, the props and coalface being lit by miners' lamps. Displays showed gas manufacture
and the uses of coal by-products, including drugs, plastics, tar, pitch and creosote, as well as film shows and
models illustrating the uses of coal. Miss Carr toured the exhibition with the Mayor, Councillor Perotti, and
met two miners who could no longer work because of ill health.

Following Fulham Borough Council's decision to implement the 1956 Clean Air Act and make the whole
borough a smoke-control area, a Clean Air Exhibition was held at Fulham Town Hall from 28 October to 2
November 1957. Invitations were distributed to each of the 3,729 dwellings in the first proposed smoke-control
area. Despite a big publicity campaign only 1,317 of the borough's residents attended the exhibition, which
showed a wide range of radiant and storage heaters, cookers and water heaters. Plans were made for a further
exhibition to be held the following year at Fulham Baths so that a larger range of appliances could be displayed.

A ticklish moment at the unveiling of a sculpture by Dr Karel Vogel outside St Peter's Church, facing the Great West Road. The untitled work in concrete was commissioned by the LCC and unveiled on 16 October 1959 by the Vice-Chairman of the LCC, Councillor Edward E. Woods. Much controversy surrounded the work, which was described variously as a 'modern monstrosity', 'an insult to women' and a 'moon' woman. There was a story that Leon Goossens, the oboist, 'had tried to recapture the position of the figure by stretching over a sitting room chair . . .'. Today the sculpture is barely seen by motorists speeding past on their way into London.

South Park was officially opened on Whit Monday, 25 May 1904, a pleasant day for 'the quiet little ceremony'. The ceremony was performed by the Mayor, Councillor John Curtis. The park was built on land known as Southfields, which Miss Charlotte Sulivan, of Broom House, had sold to Fulham Borough Council in 1903 for £1,500 an acre. The final cost of the 21 acre park was £46,000, of which £30,000 was contributed by the LCC. There had been some opposition to the park, mainly from Mr Nicholls, the well-known local builder, who said: 'I consider it would spoil Wandsworth Bridge Road if we bought the land and turned it into a park. I think the neighbourhood wants more houses in it.'

These two photographs of celebrations for the Queen's Silver Jubilee in June 1977 show four jolly policemen at Aspen Gardens and races in Tabor Road. Services of thanksgiving for the Jubilee were held, streets decorated and fêtes, flower shows, concerts, sports competitions and street parties organized. The Hammersmith Silver Jubilee Committee was set up to coordinate events around the borough. Their information sheet for street party organizers gave details of firms that could supply flags, banners and pennants, photographs, novelties, balloons, and souvenirs. The supply of trestle tables and chairs proved to be a problem and arrangements were made for schools in the borough to make them available where possible. The decorations in Protheroe Road were so good that they won the residents a prize of £1,000 in a national competition, sponsored by the *Illustrated London News*, for the best-decorated street. The prize money was used to buy guide dogs for two local blind people. Some of the flags which decorated Protheroe Road had been saved from King George V's Jubilee in 1935. Photographs of the decorations in this road and also Mirabel Road were featured in a book by Patrick Ward entitled *Flags Flying*.

Chapter 10
Leisure Pursuits &
Entertainment

Performers recreate the story of the foundation of Iona by Columba in AD 563, in the English Church Pageant held at Fulham Palace, 10–16 June 1909. As the pageant proved to be popular, performances were extended for three days. A cast of 4,000 participated in the event, which began at 3 p.m. and finished, after a break, at midnight. Many parishes from all over London provided actors and costumes for the different scenes, which were coordinated by the Pageant Master, Hugh Moss. The stand could accommodate 7,000 persons. The opening performance, on an extremely wet day, was attended by royalty and the Archbishop of Canterbury. All monies raised were to be devoted to the work of the Church.

The three exhibition centres in the borough, White City, Earls Court and Olympia, have added colour and fun to its twentieth-century history. The first exhibition at Earls Court was the America Exhibition of 1887, which included Buffalo Bill's Wild West Show. The site, on surplus railway land and only partly in the borough, was laid out as an open-air exhibition area, and featured the Great Wheel, a local landmark between 1895 and 1907. Imre Kiralfy (1845–1919), the great Hungarian exhibitions maestro, was Director General of Exhibitions at Earls Court 1895–1914, mounting shows such as the Golden West Exhibition, the Balkan States and the Military Exhibitions. In the interwar period the site was rebuilt as a more permanent exhibition centre. The Empress Hall, which was used for events such as ice hockey, boxing and musicals, was replaced by the 22-storey Empress State Building office block in 1962, and Earls Court 2 was built on the Hammersmith and Fulham side of the boundary, 1989–91. The Grand Hall at Olympia, which covered an area of 4 acres, was opened in 1886 on land once occupied by Lee and Kennedy's nursery. The venue became famous for its circuses, including Barnum and Bailey's and Bertram Mills'. From 1901 Imre Kiralfy produced spectacles at Olympia such as 'Venice in London', and it later hosted the Motor Show, the International Horse Show, and the *Daily Mail* Ideal Home Exhibition. The National Hall and Empire Hall were added in 1923 and 1929.

The White City, of which little now remains, was built on a 140-acre farmland site 1907/8, and took its name from the white façades of the buildings, which were covered with plaster mouldings. It was built for the Franco-British Exhibition of 1908, another creation of Imre Kiralfy, and consisted of some 20 palaces, 120 smaller buildings, water features and special amusements like the Mountain Scenic Railway and the Flip-Flap. Among the attractions were the Machinery Hall, the Women's Work Palace, the Indian Palace, the Palace of French Applied Art, and Ballymaclinton, a recreated Irish village. The Franco-British ran from 14 May to 31 October 1908, and was attended by 8,400,000 people. Later exhibitions at the White City included the Japan-British Exhibition, 1910, and the Latin-British Exhibition, 1912. The White City never recaptured its former glory after the First World War, although the British Industries Fair was held there in the 1920s and '30s. The LCC acquired a large part of the site in 1936 for the White City estate, and BBC Television Centre was built on another 13 acres in Wood Lane in 1949. The Shepherds Bush Exhibition Ltd company was finally wound up in 1963, and in 1994 a consortium of companies announced plans to redevelop 40 acres of the site, mainly as a shopping and leisure complex.

The stadium at the White City has also played an important part in the borough's sporting life. Built for the 1908 Olympic Games, it later hosted greyhound racing, speedway, boxing, athletics, the bizarre sport of cheetah racing, and international horse shows. The stadium closed in 1984 and was demolished soon after. West London Stadium at Wormwood Scrubs, now renamed Linford Christie Stadium, has been the venue for many athletics meetings. Rowing and sculling clubs such as the London Corinthian Sailing Club are still active on the river, and the University Boat Race, which covers a distance of about 4 miles from Putney Bridge to Mortlake, is usually lost or won on the loop of the river from Hammersmith Bridge to Chiswick Eyot. Hurlingham Club, formerly famous as a polo ground, and Queen's Club, specializing in tennis, provide exclusive sporting opportunities for their members. The most popular spectator sport of the century has been football, and the borough has three professional clubs within its boundaries. Fulham Football Club, founded in 1879, took over the site of the ruined Craven Cottage in 1896, and turned professional two years later. They were promoted to the old First Division in 1959, and are currently in the First Division (formerly the Second Division). Premier League Chelsea, at Stamford Bridge, were founded in 1905, and have had considerable success, being League Champions in 1955, FA Cup winners in 1970 and 1997, and winners of the European Cup Winners Cup in 1971. First Division Queen's Park Rangers were founded in 1886 but did not find a permanent home at Loftus Road until 1917. They won the League Cup in 1967 and were promoted to the old First Division in 1983.

There are now far fewer theatres and cinemas in the borough than there were in the early years of the twentieth century. The Lyric Theatre in King Street, first opened in 1888, still exists within a late-1970s structure, retaining much of its Victorian plasterwork inside. The Riverside Studios and the Bush Theatre also still flourish, but the Grand Theatre at Putney Bridge and the Granville Theatre of Varieties at Walham Green were demolished in 1957/8 and 1971. The King's Theatre and the Hammersmith Palace have gone, but the Shepherds Bush Empire, opened in 1903 as a music hall, is now a venue for rock concerts. In the early 1900s there were several cinemas in both Fulham and Hammersmith, some of them short-lived, and others were built in the 1920s and '30s, the heyday of the cinema when half the population used to go to the pictures at least once a week. All have closed and been demolished or turned into bingo halls or similar, such as the Gaumont Palace Cinema in Hammersmith, which is now the Apollo, a venue for live theatre and concerts. The Virgin Cinema in King Street (formerly the Regal) is the only functioning cinema in the borough. The world-famous Hammersmith Palais in Shepherds Bush Road also closed in 1997, but is now being refurbished prior to reopening. Opened in 1919, it was then a large and luxurious dance hall, with a maple floor which could accommodate 2,000 dancers. Pubs still exist in large numbers, although not as many as there used to be, but in the last few years many have been bought by brewery chains. The marketing men have changed their names and refurbished them to appeal to a younger customer group. Smart bars and restaurants are now very much part of the local scene in the wealthier parts of the borough, their arrival a result of the rise in property prices.

An aerial view of the Dahomey village at the Imperial International Exhibition at White City, 1909. The various exhibitions at White City included villages recreated in order to demonstrate different cultures, in which the residents lived as normally as possible while at the same time being on display to the crowds. An extra fee had to be paid to enter the villages, which were all carefully screened off from the other attractions. In addition to the Dahomey village, where one could see demonstrations of cookery, music making and dancing, there was also a Scottish village and an Irish village.

The Irish village Ballymaclinton was built for the Franco-British Exhibition at the White City in 1908 and was used in later exhibitions. It contained realistic reproductions of many historic buildings, including the Round Tower of Old Kilcullen, a Galway fisherman's cottage, and the abbey at Donaghmore. A number of Irish 'colleens' lived in the village and could be seen working at embroidery, carpets, lace and other rural crafts. The village had its own fire brigade staffed by the women, who were drilled by Joe Mason, a well-known fire inspector, who can be seen on the left of the photograph. Profits from the village went to fight 'consumption in Ireland, where it has made such frightful ravages'.

The motor race track at the Imperial International Exhibition, 1909. At that time few people would have had the opportunity of travelling in a motor vehicle, so this entertainment must have been of interest and amusement to many, even though the vehicles ran on a fixed track. Behind the track, work can be seen in progress on the Alpine Excelsior Railway. This was one of several railways that visitors were able to enjoy over the years at the White City. It seems only to have been in operation for about a year.

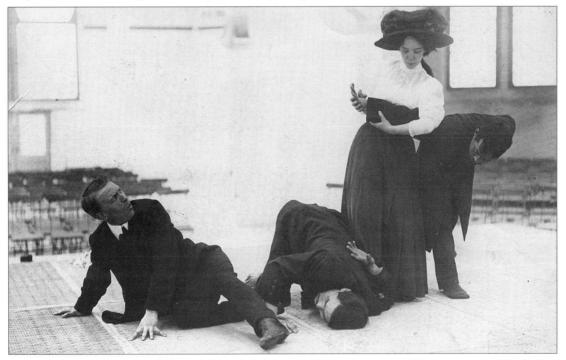

The Japan-British Exhibition held at the White City in 1910 featured a series of Japanese gardens, including the Garden of Peace, the Garden of the Floating Isle and miniature landscape gardens from the city of Tokyo. They contained lakes and islands connected by bridges, temples and houses with bushes and trees from Japan. There were Japanese entertainments such as Sumo wrestling and troupes of actors, acrobats, jugglers and dancers. There were also three villages: Formosan, Uji and Ainu. Demonstrations of ju jitsu were given and this photograph shows 'the manner in which a weak person may master a stronger'. This was so popular that it was repeated the following year at the Coronation Exhibition.

This grandiose façade, at the eastern end of Uxbridge Road and Shepherds Bush Green, formed one of the two principal entrances to the exhibitions at White City. Pictured here in 1935 at the time of a British Industries Fair, this entrance and the one in Wood Lane were designed by a young Frenchman, René Patouillard-Demoriane, for the 1908 Franco-British Exhibition. The exhibition was intended to display and promote the industrial achievements, arts and crafts of the two participating countries, and Imre Kiralfy, who had been very successfully involved with the exhibitions at Earls Court, was called on with three others to create it. Up to 12,000 workmen were employed on the 140 acre site from January 1907 until shortly after the exhibition opened in May 1908. The buildings, made of steel and concrete covered with plaster, were painted white and had fancy mouldings. Behind the Uxbridge Road entrance were a series of high-level exhibition halls, each about 70 ft wide and 400 ft long, which were built 30 ft above the ground and led to the main site in Wood Lane. Some of these halls still survive in 1999 but may be demolished as part of the latest White City development scheme. Many of the buildings were put to military use during the First World War and then became the venue for the British Industries Fairs 1921–37.

Olympia has been the scene of many exhibitions, events and spectacles since the opening of the first of its exhibition halls in 1884. Extensions made in 1895, 1923 and 1929 resulted in a space covering ½ million sq. ft. The first Motor Show was held at Olympia in 1905 and the first International Horse Show in 1907. Regular events have included the Ideal Home Exhibition, Bertram Mills' Circus, and Cruft's Dog Show. *The Miracle*, a 'wordless mystery spectacle', was staged here in 1911 by C.B. Cochran; the top photograph shows the scene in which a cripple is cured before the shrine of the Madonna. The show was produced by Max Reinhardt and the music was composed by Engelbert Humperdinck.

The centre photograph, taken during the 1958 *Daily Mail* Ideal Home Exhibition, shows the Round House and the Roof House, designed by Dr Ludowici. The Round House was completely self-contained and fully equipped for two people. The refrigerator, set into the curved entrance door, ran on paraffin and the cooker operated on bottled gas. The bottom illustration shows the dining room in Heath Robinson's house, The Gadget, at the 1934 Ideal Home Exhibition. The couple, Mr and Mrs Glowmutton, can be seen descending to their breakfast in a scene reminiscent of Nick Park's *Wallace and Gromit* cartoons. The exhibition, founded in 1908 as a publicity tool for the *Daily Mail*, has always been a showcase for furniture, interior decoration, home equipment and gadgets. The last of the Ideal Home Exhibitions at Olympia was held in 1979, after which, needing a larger venue, the exhibition moved to Earls Court.

The Golden West and American (USA) Industries Exhibition at Earls Court in 1909 was similar to the Franco-British Exhibition held at White City the previous year or indeed to earlier exhibitions at Earls Court. There was a good mixture of entertainment and education to be had. One could visit the South Dakota Caverns, watch a 'realistic and awesome reproduction' of the destruction of San Francisco, try out the rifle ranges or eat free samples at the stall of the Californian Fruit Canners' Association. There were bands and orchestras and dancing in the summer ballroom (seen on the left of the Midway promenade, above, and in the bottom photograph). The major entertainment of the exhibition was the *Red Man Spectacle* and *Black Hawk Massacre* which took place in the Empress Hall three times daily, tickets costing 1s to 3s (5–10p). During the performances there were exhibitions of steer roping by four cowboys from Wyoming, one of whom was Boots Smith, the Chief Cow Puncher, seen in the right-hand photograph.

The Balkan States Exhibition at Earls Court in 1907 was really two exhibitions in one. The main exhibition featured a large Balkan village with practical working exhibits by 'native workers' of carpet weaving, embroidery, flax spinning, crafts and village industries together with a 'real Balkan gipsy band' of dancers and singers. In the Empress Hall one could visit 'Old Japan' for an extra shilling (5p) and see a Nikko temple and bridge, teahouses, geisha and 'spring time in old Japan' with waterfalls, lotus pond and cherry blossom. One could also watch basket workers, fan painters, porcelain painters, Kyoto embroiderers, umbrella makers and a lantern painter, as pictured above, at work. Entertainments to be enjoyed included a helter skelter, a boat ride on underground rivers in the Balkan stalactite caverns, a gondola trip on the lake and a working salt mine; or for the more adventurous, perhaps a ride on the water chute (seen below, 1905), which had a drop of 75 ft over a distance of 700 ft, a ride in Sir Hiram Maxim's captive airship or a trip on the switchback railway.

The Military Exhibition at Earls Court in 1901 was rather more than a series of bands, as this illustration seems to imply. Music was played throughout the day and the programme included marches, dances, Gilbert & Sullivan and more serious operatic and orchestral works. Several other countries also participated in the exhibition. In the Empress Theatre a production of *China* or *The relief of the Legations*, described as an 'historical military spectacle', was performed twice daily. In addition to amusements such as the miniature railway and the Great Wheel, there was an exhibition of military items including portraits of generals, assorted weapons, models, uniforms, musical instruments, armour and relics of the Boer and other wars.

Fulham Football Club, founded in 1879, became a limited company at the end of the 1902/3 season. The signings made for the new season included Jack Fryer, pictured here, as goalkeeper and Captain. At 6 ft 2½ in he must have towered over his opponents on the field, where he was known as a brave and acrobatic player. He had a fine goal-keeping record for his club but was badly injured at the end of the 1906/7 season, soon after which he turned to training. When he retired in 1910 he became the licensee of The Rising Sun at 477 Fulham Road, near Stamford Bridge, but maintained links with the club until his death in December 1933.

Ian Morgan scores for Queen's Park Rangers in their 5–1 victory against Leyton Orient on 3 October 1970. The thrilling game was played in front of a crowd of 14,500. Morgan scored twice in this match, as did his teammate Rodney Marsh, the other goal being a penalty scored by Terry Venables. The team finished in eleventh place in Division 2 which 'summed up a forgettable season', the main highlight of which had been the discovery of the goal-keeping talent of Phil Parkes who came from Walsall and remained for eight years.

Scenes of jubilation greeted the players of Chelsea Football Club after they won the FA Cup for the first time in 65 years in 1970. They finally won 2–1 against Leeds after extra time in a replay at Old Trafford, Manchester, on 20 April 1970. They had previously drawn against their opponents at Wembley earlier in the month. A civic reception hosted by the Mayor, Alderman Seton Forbes-Cockell, was held for the team at Fulham Old Town Hall the following day. Several thousand of the club's supporters turned up to see the arrival of their heroes with an escort of police outriders on motor cycles. The colours blue and white were to be seen everywhere.

The White City stadium, built to house the 1908 Olympics, was officially inaugurated by King Edward VII on 13 July l908. A crowd of some 30,000 spectators viewed the ceremony, in which over 2,000 sportsmen and sportswomen participated. Among them were 'twenty Danish ladies in neat gymnastic costume' (some of whom are pictured here) who gave one of the non-competitive displays which were open to women. Their clothing, made of cream serge with light-brown hose, was much admired, and contrasted favourably with the conventional navy blue with scarlet or white trimmings of the English team. The aerial view of the stadium was taken in about 1949 when work on building Wolfe House (the L-shaped block to the left of the stadium) was under way and a horse show, possibly the International Horse Show, was in progress. Prior to the Second World War this event had been held at Olympia but after the cessation of hostilities it resumed at the White City. The stadium, scene of many sporting events including greyhound racing, boxing, speedway, baseball and athletics, was closed in September 1984 and demolished almost immediately.

The open-air swimming pool adjacent to Wormholt Park, *c.* 1923. The site was chosen with a view to relieving the congestion at Lime Grove Baths and to providing work for the unemployed. The Borough Engineer and Surveyor, R. Hampton Clucas, designed the pool, which took sixty men six months to build. It was 150 ft long and 75 ft wide with a maximum depth of just over 7 ft and held 337,500 gallons of water. Lawns and changing facilities surrounded the pool. The official opening took place on 4 August 1923, with exhibitions of swimming and diving.

The Oxford crew preparing to compete in the 71st Oxford and Cambridge University Boat Race on 28 March 1914. Cambridge won the race by 4½ lengths in 20 minutes and 23 seconds, their first win after five years of defeat. Because of the First World War, the race was not contested again until 1920. Some schools kept up rowing as best they could during the war years but there were no oarsmen left at either Oxford or Cambridge to compete. Forty-two 'blues' lost their lives in the conflict.

Polo ponies at the Hurlingham Club, *c.* 1905. Frank Heathcote founded the Hurlingham Club as a pigeon-shooting club in 1869. It was realized that this sport alone was not enough to attract new members, so polo was introduced and played at the club from June 1874. From then until 1939, when it ceased to be played there, the club was the headquarters of English polo and in its heyday there was stabling for 50 coach horses and 200 polo ponies. Pigeon shooting was abandoned in 1905 after a lawsuit between those to wished to continue shooting and those who considered it a barbaric pastime.

The bar of the old George at Hammersmith Broadway on the day of its closure, 18 August 1911. It was demolished as part of a road-widening scheme that involved the building of its successor to the rear. Several nearby buildings were also demolished. When the new pub designed by Messrs Newell Parr & Kates opened, only the ground floor bars were complete.

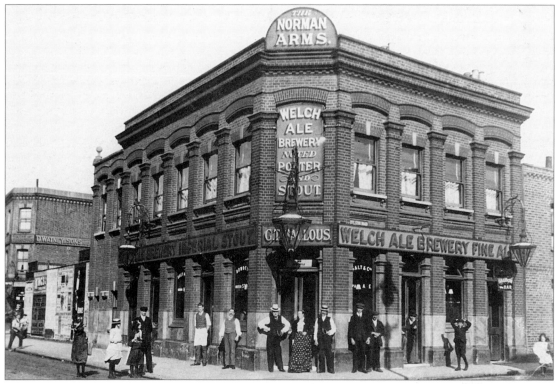

The Norman Arms, on the corner of Lillie Road and Rylston Road, c. 1910, was the second pub of that name on the site. A mid-nineteenth century beerhouse there was rebuilt c. 1881 and again in 1963. In 1860 John Smith, a beer retailer, applied for a licence to sell spirits at his house in Crown Lane (now Lillie Road). This was rejected because the house was 'comparatively small and inconvenient, and though fit for a beerhouse, was most decidedly unfit for the house of a licensed victualler'. In his support it was stated that 'there were 39 houses tenanted [nearby] by labouring men and others, who required spirits, and could not get them without considerable difficulty.'

Built as a variety theatre for the theatrical impresario Oswald Stoll, the Shepherds Bush Empire is seen here in September 1953 just before its closure and conversion into the BBC Television Theatre. With two shows a night, the outgoing audience of the 2,332 capacity theatre could not, for safety reasons, come into contact with the incoming audiences, so the famous designer Frank Matcham built entrances on one side of the theatre and exits on the other. The opening night, scheduled for 17 August 1903, was postponed until the following evening as 'a lynx-eyed minion of the London County Council . . . discovered that the word "exit" did not appear on a certain door'. The house capacity was oversubscribed the following night.

A performance of *See How They Run* at the King's Theatre, Hammersmith Road, in the week commencing 28 February 1949. This popular West End play had already been seen at the King's in 1946 and 1948. It was performed by the Carl Bernard Company, which regularly held seasons here, usually in the summer months, as part of the Season of West End Successes. The theatre, which had opened on Boxing Day 1902 with the pantomime *Cinderella*, closed after the final performance of *Dick Whittington and His Cat*, starring Anne Ziegler and George Doonan, on 29 January 1955. It was demolished in 1963 after a short period of use as a television

The Granville Theatre of Varieties, Walham Green, *c.* 1905. This was the brainchild of four theatre people including Dan Leno, who having managed two other theatres thought it might be interesting and profitable to open their own music hall. Frank Matcham designed the theatre, which held 1,122. The commemoration stone was laid on 1 September 1898 amid great hilarity, according to contemporary reports, and the theatre opened 18 days later. Many great names of the era trod its boards, including Harry Champion, George Robey, Little Tich and Marie Lloyd. The theatre closed on 11 December 1954, was used for a time as a television recording studio and then demolished, after much protest, in December 1971.

The Lyric Theatre, Bradmore Grove, Hammersmith, during demolition, 19 June 1972. The Lyric Theatre had opened on 20 July 1895, replacing an earlier structure. The tiny new theatre was designed by Frank Matcham and had a seating capacity of only 775 people. It was enlarged slightly four years later. In the 1970s much of the surrounding area was redeveloped, which necessitated large-scale demolition of shops and homes and the relocation of the theatre and Hammersmith Market. The Queen opened the new Lyric Theatre, built within the new shopping and housing development off King Street, on 18 October 1979.

A dance competition, to the music of Lou Praeger and his band, at the Hammersmith Palais, 1949. The Palais opened at the end of 1919 in a converted roller-skating rink which had been fitted up in a 'luxurious and charming' manner to the designs of Bertie Crew. Apart from the period 1929–33, when it was used as an ice rink, it provided a popular dance venue for west London until closure in 1997. It is expected to reopen in September 1999. Non-dancers were also catered for, with a promenade from which they could look down and view the proceedings. Two daily sessions were held and details of the hours and prices can still be seen painted on the rear wall of the Palais from Hammersmith Broadway Station.

Index